the calling
of a generation

Evangeline Weiner

Christine,
Go forth!
God has new things!
Evangeline
Psalm 2:8

maranatha *M* publications

Over 30 years of publishing

A Maranatha Book
2009

Published by Maranatha Publications
P.O. Box 1799
Gainesville, Florida 32602
(352) 375-6000
www.weinermedia.com

Contact the author:
Evangeline@weinermedia.com
www.callingofageneration.com

Book Design and Cover Photography and Design
by Erik Hollander

Library of Congress Catalogue-in-Publication Data:
LC Control Number 2007 061222

ISBN 0-938558-40-4 (Hardcover)
ISBN 0-938558-43-9 (Paperback)

Dedication

This book is dedicated to all those men and women of faith who have gone before us—those who have sacrificed their lives for the Gospel and laid the foundations for what we have and understand today.

I also dedicate this book to my parents, Bob and Rose Weiner, who never let me live an ordinary life, and included my siblings, Stephanie, John, and Catherine, and me in all their adventures in the ministry. You both always wanted us right up front doing it with you. Without you both, I wouldn't be who I am today. Dad, you taught me what faith really is and you are my biggest cheerleader. Mom, you always have wisdom for me and never let me set a standard for myself that is less than giving God my everything. Thank you both for your help with some of the chapters of this book. You both are my heroes, and I love you!

To my grandparents, Dr. Henry and Grace Russell, who have spent over the last fifty years as ministers in the Methodist Church—you both have shown me the greatest example of the true love of Jesus and having fun in life! Also to the late Robert Weiner, who was raised in a Jewish home and came to know Jesus as his Messiah shortly after my dad was born, who always wanted to be about his heavenly Father's business—thank you for all your daily prayers for me and all the family to find God's will and blessing for our lives. And to Geri Weiner, my grandmother—you are my little evangelist and I love you!

contents

introduction

chapters

why this generation
is so important to god

Over the past few years, I have had a real burden to see this generation of Christian young people rise up in faith and fulfill their calling. I have seen young people with a genuine calling from God who want to change the world.

Yet, I have watched them after they have graduated from their various universities, schools, or internships, and regardless of where they live, they are not sure what to do next. They flounder for a while, and then just get caught up in the status quo of making a living. They give up their dreams and settle for a routine existence of going to church and trying to be a good, successful person—the kingdom of God suffers from this loss.

This book was written out of a burden to see young people—no matter what their field of endeavor—released into the Harvest to fulfill the mandate of Jesus to change the world, make disciples of all nations, and see Christ's great kingdom come on earth as it is in heaven.

To do this Christians must get beyond the narrow box of separating the secular and the spiritual and take over the mountains of influence that form nations—Church and Family/ Government and Law/ Media, Arts and Entertainment/ Education/ Finances, Marketplace and Business/ Architecture and Engineering/ Science, Medicine, Invention and Discovery.

God wants His children to be co-laborers with Him. Without God, we can do nothing, and without people, God will do nothing. A story is told about a farmer that illustrates this point. A man bought a farm that was run down. The soil was full of weeds and the ground was full of chuckholes. The man labored for a long time. He pulled the weeds, filled the holes, fertilized the soil, planted seed, irrigated the land and finally, the farm began to produce a good crop. A friend stopped by, and astonished at the transformation exclaimed, "Wow! It is amazing what God has done with this farm." The farmer responded, "Well, you should have seen it when God had it all to Himself."

The first command that God gave Adam and Eve in the garden was to cultivate the earth and to take dominion of it. When Jesus brought redemption to the human race and became "the Firstborn of many brethren" and as the Second Adam and the Father of the New Creation, He reemphasized the dominion mandate, commissioning His followers to make disciples of all nations. Jesus didn't send angels to preach the Gospel, He sent people.

The Generation of Jesus—The Promised Seed

The future will be what we will make it, and what it will be depends on our response to His call. We cannot underestimate the call of God on this generation. The devil has done his best to destroy us through abortion, drugs, sexually transmitted diseases, violence, divorce and rejection by parents.

There have been two other significant times in history when Satan has inspired the murder of innocent babes. When Moses was born, the devil tried to destroy "the deliverer" by exciting Pharaoh to kill all the male infants of a tribe. When Jesus was born, the devil excited Herod to murder all the infants of a city from two-years-old and under in his attempt to kill the King of Israel.

Since 1973 in the United States, the devil has been destroying the unborn through abortion in the greatest genocide in history. Following our example, other nations have adopted this practice. In the United States alone, the tens of millions of infants who have been murdered is a number equivalent to a people group larger than the size of the entire nation of Canada. [1]

In Moses' day in order to get one man, the devil inspired the slaughter of the infants of a tribe. In Jesus' day, Satan inspired the murder of all the infants in a city to kill the promised Savior. Is he after the promised seed again? Think of the magnitude of the seed Satan has been trying to destroy. Could it be there is not just one person the enemy is after, but instead a whole nation of deliverers that Jesus wants to release for world harvest to bring His kingdom on earth as it is in heaven? I believe that there is!

The good news is Satan didn't get Moses, he didn't get Jesus, and he hasn't gotten the promised seed of this generation who are destined to bring in the greatest harvest of souls for the kingdom of God that the world has ever seen.

Are you one of the promised seed God has called to turn the world upside down for the cause of Christ? The very fact that you are reading this book tells me that you are. Although this book is written especially for the younger members of the body of Christ, there are many Joshuas and Calebs who have been waiting and praying to see this day. I want to encourage you as well. God will use all those who will embrace the promises of God and refuse to give themselves over to disobedience and unbelief. The sons of God are all those, regardless of age or gender, who are giving themselves to be led by His Holy Spirit (Rom. 8:14).

Are you ready to embark on a journey to follow the Lord in full surrender of self? Are you ready to stop seeking what is acceptable or normal for society, to give up seeking the praises of men, and regardless of the cost, look to God and believe Him to use you to alter the course of your nation and world history forever? If you aren't now, I believe when you finish reading this book you will be!

DREAMING GOD'S DREAMS

The main purpose of this book is to build faith, and to teach and encourage believers to enter the joy of the Lord by experiencing life in Christ through complete abandon to Him. This book features testimonies of young people who have done just that. Through their friendship and fellowship with the Lord, these young people have been filled with dreams from God, and they have already done something with them.

Between their stories, I have included teachings on the importance and great blessing of self-surrender to the Lordship of Jesus, practical ways to develop your faith and your relationship with the Lord, as well as a vision for Christ's dominion in the nations. My prayer is that you are encouraged to live your life from the dreams and desires born in your heart through your fellowship with the Father.

When Jesus came, God changed human history forever—a new world began for the human race. Isaiah prophesied about Jesus' mission, "I will give You as a covenant to the people, as a light to the Gentiles, to open blind eyes, to bring out prisoners from the prison, those who sit in darkness from the prison house…New things I declare; before they spring forth I tell you of them" (Isa. 42:6,7-9).

The prophetic promise given to Jesus and all those who follow Him in sonship is recorded by David, "Only ask, and I will give the nations as your inheritance, the whole earth as your possession" (Psalm 2:7). When Jesus rose from the dead, I believe He knelt down and in His redeeming blood, wrote, "Mine! I claim every nation!" He sent the Holy Spirit and commissioned His people to go and work in the power of His Spirit to "make disciples of all nations" and promised that He would be there working with them "always, to the end of the world" (Matt. 28:18-20). If you are a believer you have been given the call to do your part to fulfill this Great Commission through the power of the Risen Christ—regardless of the field of endeavor or mountain of influence that God has called you to affect.

A Vessel for the Creative Power of God

God is creating constantly. He is creating new things for His people to do right now to cause "His blessing to flow as far as the curse is found."[2] Isaiah writes of God's creative power, and about the new things God will do saying, "Behold, I will do a new thing, now it shall spring forth; shall you not know it?... I have made you hear new things from this time, even hidden things, and you did not know them. They are created *now* and not from the beginning" (Isa. 43:19, 48: 6b-7). God wants His children to bring forth these "new things" in the earth through the power of His Holy Spirit.

My prayer is that you are encouraged to rise up in faith and in the power of the Holy Spirit to see your dreams become reality. The Scriptures exhort us to "imitate those who through faith and patience have inherited the promises" (Heb. 6:12). The true stories in this book furnish just such examples in faith. They are inspiring, instructive, and adventurous and are written by young people who have stepped out in faith in total abandon to God and His purposes and have seen Him do the impossible.

A few years ago, when I felt the Holy Spirit tug on my heart and ask me to write this book, I thought about it for a second and then I began to offer my objections. I wondered what in the world I would write about the subject that people didn't already know since I was only 19-years-old at that time. I told the Lord about all my inadequacies. "What would I put on the back of the book about what I do that would make people think I had anything to say?" Finally I told the Lord, "After thinking this over, I don't really want to do it."

Immediately the Lord spoke to my heart and said, "Okay, Evangeline, I will ask someone else to do it." My heart felt like a lighting bolt hit it. I didn't want to miss out on what the Lord wanted me to do. Without any other hesitation I said, "Okay, Lord, I change my mind. I will do it—I want to do it." Within minutes the

Lord gave me the entire plan for this book. I knew that this wasn't just a good idea—this was a God idea!

LIVING IN THE REALM OF THE IMPOSSIBLE

One important thought—when God calls you to do something, it will probably be impossible. That is, impossible to do in your own ability. If you are sure you have the ability to get it done, you can act and take the credit. You can pat yourself on the back for a job well done. It takes no faith. You can tell everyone what you have done for the Lord. But when you know you can't do it, and you step out in faith and trust in God to work through you, you will tap into His supernatural power and ability. You will give Him all the glory.

In your own strength, you can spend your life working hard gathering wealth, creating new inventions, or developing new business strategies. You can try very hard to achieve something great. You can have an impressive strategy mapped out and follow it faithfully.

You may be successful, but you could end up becoming like the rich man Jesus told about who was very prosperous and was rejoicing because he had stored up food and possessions to last him for many years so that he could retire and live it up. But God said to him, "You fool! This very night your soul is required of you; and now who will own what you have prepared?" God called him a fool. Jesus pointed out his sin—he had laid up "treasure for himself and was not rich toward God" (Luke 12:21).

On the other hand you can say, "God, I am nothing, I don't know how to do very much, but here are all my gifts and talents, and more than that, here is my entire life—do with it whatever you want." Within an hour, or even in minutes, God can give you a plan that could change the course of history, a plan that you would have never thought of on your own. He is the God of the impossible!

And you can be sure that the thing God will call you to do will eventually be beyond what you are capable of doing in your own strength and effort, and will be impossible to do without God's power and anointing. Faith will be required to accomplish it.

Testimony to the truth that the impossible is accomplished by faith and trust in God is found throughout the pages of scripture. Hebrews reminds us that it was *by faith* that those who looked to God for power and victory "subdued kingdoms, worked righteousness, obtained promises, stopped the mouths of lions, quenched the violence of fire, escaped the edge of the sword, out of weakness were made strong, became valiant in battle, turned to flight the armies of the enemy" (Heb.11:33-34).

CHANGING HISTORY

As you read the chapters and the stories of young people like you who said "yes" to what the Lord was calling them to do, I pray that faith floods your heart and causes you to become a man or woman of strength and courage, ready to fight and win our generation and change the world for Jesus Christ! No matter what your age, you can make your life count for the kingdom of God.

When all the other Israelites were hiding in caves from the Midianites, Gideon, though small in his own eyes, was threshing his wheat in the wine press and guarding it so the Midianites could not steal it. Seeing his brave spirit, the Angel of the Lord appeared to him and said, "The Lord is with you, you mighty man of valor…Go in this might of yours, and you shall save Israel from the hand of the Midianites. Have I not sent you?" (Judges 6:12,14).

Even after this angelic visitation, Gideon did not believe that he could do it. However, after being convinced of God's direction, Gideon went forward in obedience to God's instuctions, trusting not in himself, but in God—and he conquered Israel's enemies and brought great deliverance!

If you read this book with expectation and an eager heart to surrender yourself to be everything that God has called you to be— if you are willing to obey the Holy Spirit no matter what the cost— then you can live a life that changes history! As you answer God's call, you will discover as Gideon did that the power is not in who you are, but in "who He is."

As you follow Jesus' call to go and make disciples of all nations, Jesus promised, "I will always be with you to the end of time." As you obey the call of God to "go in this your might"—the might of the Holy Spirit— you will overcome the enemy and usher the kingdom of God into the hearts of men, women, children and ultimately nations. Step out in faith and answer God's call. Take your place on the battle-field— your Captain waits to give you His orders!

ಐ ೋ ೈ ೞ

A Personal Note to You

Dear Reader,

Will you do me a favor? I would love to hear your comments. Please visit me at The Calling of a Generation on facebook and share your thoughts and ideas with me, or email me at Evangeline@weinermedia.com.

Follow me on twitter.com/EvangelineW.

Look forward to seeing you there!

Evangeline Weiner

chapter 1

ESCAPING THE FATE OF A NOWHERE MAN

> I have never even considered the direction.
> For where am I to go? And by what shall I steer?
> What is to be my quest?
>
> —FRODO BAGGINS
> J.R.R. TOLKIEN, *THE LORD OF THE RINGS*

We were born to be dreamers. In "trailing clouds of glory,"[1] God sends each of us to earth for a purpose—with a dream in our heart—our own personal blueprint from the Master Architect. Before the prison house of doubt and unbelief began to box us in, as children we beheld the light and glory in the place of dreaming. Nowhere is the capacity to dream more alive than in the heart of a child.

Go with me into any first grade class to the dreaming place and what do you hear? You hear their dreams. A little girl with rosy cheeks speaks up, "I'm going to be an astronaut and a lawyer!" "I'm going to be the President of the United States of America!" a bright-eyed boy shouts. A tiny girl with curly, blonde hair giggles, "When I grow up I'm going to a famous actress!" "I'm going to be a doctor," a small boy with glasses says seriously. Zookeeper, fireman, lion trainer, policeman, basketball star, inventor—the list goes on and on. Children believe they can be anything they want to be.

Fast-forward a few years. Enter the sixth grade classroom. The same kids in the first grade class are there, but something has changed. The bright-eyed boy, taller and thinner now, has held on to his dream in all his childhood innocence. He yells, "I am going to be the President of the United States of America!" The whole classroom laughs and points fingers. Then even the teacher chuckles as he pats Johnny on the back and says, "Sure you will, son. Wouldn't we all like to be someone great?"

For one of the first times in his life, Johnny gets very discouraged and begins to wonder what in the world he was thinking by dreaming he could be the President. He begins to talk himself out of his dream, as the kids continue pointing at him and mockingly call him a dreamer.

By the time Johnny enters high school, his dream of being the President—once so vivid—has vanished into a slight memory. He has listened to the lies of doubt and unbelief and finds many reasons to convince himself that he is not good enough, not skilled enough, not smart enough. "Guess what I used to think I could be?" Johnny laughs, as he remembers that he actually believed he could do something that mattered.

As Johnny passes into adult life, unbelief, fear, doubt, and worry are now the stones that clog his channel to the Divine. These attitudes, left unresolved, are certain to keep Johnny from discovering or fulfilling God's dream and plans for his life and will instead paint a negative picture of the things he fears, which can easily become his reality.

GOD'S ETERNAL PURPOSE

Do you remember dreaming as a child? I do. I loved to sit and think of all the awesome things that God was going to use me to do when I grew up. I also dreamed about what God was going to use me to do while I was still a child. I really believed it was all going to happen and I still do.

Maybe some of you once thought that you were going to be a millionaire, a politician, a news anchor, a researcher who would find the cure for cancer, a founder of orphanages, the next Mother Teresa, or maybe a missionary to Africa. Whatever the dream was, it was probably something big. When you were young there were no little dreams and nothing seemed impossible or too great to be accomplished. It is this childlike attitude that Jesus told us to imitate. He reminded His disciples, "I say to you, whoever does not receive the kingdom of God as a little child will not enter it at all" (Luke 18:16-17 NAS). Maintaining this childlike spirit is so important Jesus tells us that without it we cannot enter the kingdom.

Not all dreams of childhood or adult life are from God, but it is important to keep the capacity to dream alive so we can dream the dreams inspired by the Holy Spirit. One sign that the dream is from God is that it will be impossible to do without Him. Here is my question for you—as the years have gone by and you have entered the "real world," have you forgotten your dream that you could make a difference in this world? Has your life just become a life of check marks? Are you filling out life's checklist of all the important things you think are required without considering your God-ordained purpose?

It is easy to become like the group of people Jesus calls "the Gentiles," who He describes as spending their lives gathering and collecting, worrying about what they are going to eat, how they are going to become successful, where they will live, what they will wear, who they will marry, and about whatever else life throws their way. It is easy to get trapped into focusing on gathering and collecting for life's needs and to forget Jesus' admonition to "not worry about these things," but to trust God and "seek the kingdom of God first and His righteousness" with the promise that "everything you need will be given to you" (Matt. 6:31-33).

Life has got to be more than just going to a good university, establishing a good career, getting married, buying a house, a dog, a car, raising a family, retiring, and dying. These are all good things, but if you are not fulfilling a purpose greater than yourself, if God's dream is not alive in your heart, then you have failed at life and are missing out on God's great blessing.

We must realize that our lives are not meant to be insignificant, for the Apostle Paul reminds us that the whole world is "waiting to be set free from its slavery to corruption into the freedom of the glory of the children of God" (Rom. 8:21 NAS). If you entertain the thinking that you're nothing special, or you're not good enough, then God can't change the world through you, or use you to fulfill His purposes.

You are actually contradicting the promises of God, and you are agreeing with the enemy in doubt and unbelief. Satan will rob you of becoming all that God has planned for you to become, and God will not receive the glory from your life that is due Him. One more future will fall short of the plan that God has ordained. This is spiritual abortion. Your life of aimlessness will have as much meaning to the world around you and to the kingdom of God as the man described in song by the Beatles: "He's a real nowhere man, sitting in his nowhere land, doing lots of nowhere things, for nobody."

BECOMING A DREAMER

In the early 20th century when most women did not attempt to do anything outside the home, Lady Astor—the first woman ever elected to the British Parliament who championed the rights of women and children—realized the importance of having a vision. "Dreams are great," she remarked. "When they disappear you may still be here, but you will have ceased to live."[2] Isaiah said it this way,

"Without a vision, a redemptive revelation from God, the people perish" (Proverbs. 29:18 AMP).

In the 19th century, T.E. Lawrence's dreams enabled him to become a British archeological scholar, adventurer, and military strategist whose legend inspired the epic film, *Lawrence of Arabia*. His success lay in his belief not just about the dream, but the dreamer. Lawrence explained, "All people dream, but not equally. Those who dream by night in the dusty recesses of their mind, wake in the morning to find that it was vanity. But the dreamers of the day are dangerous people, for they dream their dreams with open eyes, and make them come true."[3]

Walt Disney said it this way, "All our dreams come true if we have the courage to pursue them."[4] The dreamers of the day are those who dream with faith.

What do the lives of these great people tell us? A person with a dream can accomplish something of value in this world. The great news is this—as you spend time in God's Presence, the Holy Spirit will fill your heart with God's dreams. God invites you to come into His heart of secrets, which is the fountain of all creativity, wisdom, invention, and purpose.

Pay attention to the dreams and desires that come into your heart while you are spending time in fellowship with Jesus. Don't look at yourself, at your own abilities, and your inadequacies. God doesn't ask you to work for Him in your own strength. He calls you to yield your life to Him in self-surrender, which simply means relax and follow Him—He's got it. God reminds us, "It is not by might nor by power, but by My Spirit says the Lord" (Zech. 4:6). And again, "Faithful is He who calls you, Who also will do it" (1 Thes. 5:24 NAS).

God told Jeremiah, "Before I formed you in the womb I knew you; before you were born I sanctified you; I ordained you as a prophet to the nations" (Jer. 1:5). God formed not only Jeremiah;

He also formed you in your mother's womb and created you for a purpose. What else does the Lord say? " 'I know my plans that I have for you," declares the Lord, 'plans for good and not for disaster, to give you a future and a hope' " (Jer. 29:11 NLT). Are you ready to be used by God to change your generation? He's ready to equip and release you!

ANSWERING THE CALL

One of the most important things to remember is that you are not a robot. God has not programmed you to complete your destiny automatically. Many people live and die and never fulfill God's purpose for their lives. He gives you a choice. He gives you a free will, and it is up to you to choose God's plan and obey and follow Him, or to do things your way. Jesus makes this very clear in this parable about the kingdom of God:

> The kingdom of Heaven can be illustrated by the story of a king who had prepared a great wedding feast for his son. Many guests were invited, and when the banquet was ready, he sent his servants to notify everyone that it was time to come. But they all refused! So he sent other servants to tell them, "The feast has been prepared, and choice meats have been cooked. Everything is ready. Hurry!" But the guests he had invited ignored them and went about their business, one to his farm, and another to his store.
>
> Others seized his messengers and treated them shamefully, even killing some of them. Then the king became furious. He sent out his army to destroy the murderers and burn their city.
>
> And he said to his servants, "The wedding feast is ready, and the guests I invited aren't worthy of the honor. Now go out to the street corners and invite everyone you see." So the servants

brought in everyone they could find, good and bad alike, and the banquet hall was filled with guests.

But when the king came in to meet the guests, he noticed a man who wasn't wearing the proper clothes for a wedding. "Friend," he asked, "how is it that you are here without wedding clothes?" And the man had no reply. Then the king said to his aides, "Bind him hand and foot and throw him out into the outer darkness, where there is weeping and gnashing of teeth. For many are called, but few are chosen" (Matthew 22:1-14 NLT).

From this parable, we learn that all are invited into the kingdom of God. Both the good and bad alike are accepted when they come in willing obedience. However, among those who are called, there are those who are not "found worthy of the honor." They refuse God's call because they are too busy with their own affairs. They have their own goals and plans and can't be bothered with God's call on their lives. Some people get so mad about being asked to accept God's invitation, and about being reminded that there is a King to whom they owe their allegiance, they will actually persecute, shame, and kill God's messengers.

The sure way to fulfill God's call is to obey Him. There is no such thing as a Christian who is in rebellion against God. To be a Christian is to give up your rebellion and surrender to His Lordship. Jesus taught, "If you refuse to take up your cross and follow Me, you are not worthy of being mine" (Matt. 10:38 NLT).

The parable of the wedding feast illustrates the self-centered will that runs like a gigantic fault line through the human race—and this self-centered existence keeps people from living the truly amazing life of the Spirit. All who want to follow Jesus must submit to the requirement that He laid down. Jesus told the multitudes, "If any one of you wants to be My follower, you must put aside your selfish ambition, shoulder your cross daily, and follow Me. If you try to keep your life for yourself, you will lose it. But if you give up your life for Me, you will find true life" (Luke 9:23-24 NLT).

This is what it takes to gain entrance into His kingdom. But, what an awesome promise! Full surrender allows us to sit down at the table of fellowship and the feast of resurrection life that God has prepared for those who love Him! What an invitation!

THE RIGHTEOUS ACTS OF THE SAINTS

Jesus ends this parable with a word of warning about a person who answered the king's call to come to the feast, but came without the wedding garment. Who does this man the king called "friend" represent? What wedding garment was this person missing that disqualified him from being chosen and caused him to be "cast into the place of outer darkness?" The Bible gives us the answer.

In Revelation, we catch a glimpse of the wedding clothes and another wedding banquet. This banquet is the marriage feast of "the Bride, the wife of the Lamb." John explains, "It was given to her to clothe herself in fine linen, bright and clean; *for the fine linen is the righteous acts (good deeds) of the saints*" (Rev. 19:7-8 NAS, NLT).

After this, the scene changes, the heavens open, and One appears on a white horse crowned with many diadems who is the "King of Kings and the Lord of Lords" and the armies that *follow Him* are "dressed in the purest white linen"(Rev.19:14,16).

James tells us about the righteous acts and good deeds that will clothe us if we follow Him:

> Dear brothers and sisters, what's the use of saying you have faith, if you don't prove it by your actions? That kind of faith can't save anyone. Suppose you see a brother or a sister who needs food or clothing, and you say, "Well, good-bye and God bless you; stay warm and eat well"—but then you don't give that person any food or clothing. What good does that do? So you see, it isn't enough

just to have faith. Faith that doesn't show itself by good deeds is not faith at all—it is dead and useless…

Don't you see that our ancestor Abraham was declared right with God because of what he did when he offered his son Isaac on the altar? You see, he was trusting God so much that he was willing to do whatever God told him to do. His faith was made complete by what he did—by his actions.

And so it happened just as the scriptures say: "Abraham believed God, so God declared him to be righteous." He was even called "the friend of God" so you see, we are made right with God by what we do, not by faith alone.

Rahab the prostitute is another example of this. She was made right with God by her actions—when she hid those messengers and sent them safely away by a different road (James 2:14-25 NLT).

James concludes, "So you see, faith by itself isn't enough. Unless it produces good deeds, it is dead and useless" (v 26). Good deeds are the result of loving God, spending time in His Presence and trusting and obeying Him. We will naturally perform good deeds out of our love for God because He will put His directions and desires in our heart through the inspiration of His Holy Spirit.

Having all this in mind, Peter exhorts us, "So dear brothers and sisters, work hard to prove that you really are among those God has called and chosen. Doing this, you will never stumble or fall away. And God will open wide the gates of heaven for you to enter into the eternal kingdom of our Lord and Savior Jesus Christ" (2 Peter 1:10).

RETURNING TO THE FATHER'S HOUSE

If you want to live a fulfilled and happy life and receive an eternal reward, let God use your life for His glory. Believe what God has said, and love and obey Him. If you haven't been following Jesus, don't think that it is too late for you and that you have blown it. Don't believe that you have messed up your calling forever, or that your sins have disqualified you. This is another lie of the enemy.

Here is a scripture for you, "For the gifts and the calling of God are irrevocable" (Rom.11:29). Paul explains, "We are made right with God when we trust in Jesus Christ to take away our sins. And we all can be saved in this way, no matter who we are or what we have done" (Rom. 3:22 NLT).

If you have fallen away from God, you can forsake sin and disobedience, and return to God with your whole heart. "Today is the day" and "now" is the time to return to God's purposes for your life. God's mercy and forgiveness are great. However, there is still a tragedy involved in every rebellion. That tragedy is that you have less time to serve God and do His will. So don't delay. Today is the day and now is the time to return to God and His love and His wonderful purposes for your life.

To explain the love and forgiveness of God, Jesus told the story of the prodigal son who left his Father's house and spent his inheritance on wild women and riotous living. When he came to his senses, he said: "At home, even the hired men have food enough to spare, and here I am, dying of hunger! I will go home to my father and say, 'Father, I have sinned against both heaven and you, and I am no longer worthy of being called your son. Please take me on as a hired servant.' "

When the son was still far away, his father saw him coming, and overcome with "love and compassion he ran to his son, embraced him, and kissed him… His father said to the servants, 'Bring the finest robe in the house and put it on him. Get a ring for his finger, and sandals for his feet. And kill the calf we have been fattening in the pen. We must celebrate with a feast, for this son of mine was dead and has now returned to life. He was lost, but now he is found'" (Luke 15:17-32 NLT).

To return to his father's house, the prodigal son had to make a decision and walk away from the pigpen of his own making. He had to decide in his heart to give up his freedom of self-choice to become one of his father's hired servants. This is repentance. The good news is the father received the prodigal back as more than a servant— he gave him the position of honored son.

In the same manner, Jesus came to restore the sonship with the Father that was lost in Adam and Eve's fall. He said, "I have called you friends *if you do whatever I command you*...No longer do I call you servants, for a servant does not know what his master is doing; but I have called you friends, for all things that I heard from My Father I have made known to you" (John 15:14-15). What a great privilege!

If all this has spoken to you and you know you are not where you need to be, why not surrender to the Lord. Ask Jesus to take selfish ambition out of your heart and every dream that is not from Him. Ask Jesus to give you the new birth and baptize you in the Holy Spirit—then, bury your old life in the waters of baptism.

Ask Jesus to put His dreams in your heart and to change your desires. Give Him your imagination like the blank canvas of an artist, and let Jesus paint it with His dreams for you. He will do it! Just give Him your future right now, all your hopes, aspirations, dreams—and in exchange, you will receive His plan, His aspirations, His hopes, His desires for you to affect your generation for Him! This is what is called the Great Exchange—trading your life for His life!

Now I see the crimson wave,
The fountain deep and wide;
Jesus, my Lord, my life He saves,
I see His wounded side.
Now the cleansing stream I see,

I hear the speaking blood;
I see the New Creation rise,
Out of the crimson flood.

I rise to walk in heaven's light,
Above the world and sin,
With heart made pure and garments white,
And Christ enthroned within.

Amazing grace! It's heaven below,
To feel the blood applied,
And Jesus, my Lord and Savior know,
My Jesus crucified.

—Modified from a hymn by
PHOEBE PALMER *1804-1874*

"We now have this light shining in our hearts, but we ourselves are like fragile clay jars containing this great treasure. This makes it clear that our great power is from God, not from ourselves" (2 Cor. 4:17 NLT).

chapter 2

THE PATH OF ABSOLUTE SURRENDER

What is worship—to do the will of God—that is worship.

—ISHMAEL

HERMAN MELVILLE, *MOBY DICK*

I count all things loss for the excellence of the knowledge of
Christ Jesus my Lord, for whom I have suffered the loss of all
things and count them as rubbish that I may gain Christ.

—PAUL

PHILIPPIANS 3:8

When Jennifer Miller was 16, the Lord spoke to her and said,
"Make a decision. I have had grace on your life, but the grace is
getting ready to end. You are either for Me or against Me. There is
no more middle ground." If that statement wasn't strong enough,
His next statement absolutely rocked her—"What will it be? Are
you going to serve Me, or are you going to serve yourself?"

Jennifer decided to make the "Great Exchange" and traded her
life for His! God took her from just being a college student and
used her to literally help change and influence a nation! Her story
is a testimony to the truth of God's word, "He is able to do super-
abundantly, far over and above all that we ask or think—infinitely
beyond our highest prayers, desires, thoughts, hopes, or dreams"
(Eph. 3:20 AMP).

JENNIFER'S STORY

When I was growing up, I would always hear people speaking about how God was using them and all the miraculous things that were taking place through their ministry. If I had known them personally and had the opportunity, I would have asked them to teach me how they came to operate in this miracle power.

Although I wished that I could operate in this same anointing, I always thought, "How would I ever do these things? I am just a simple person." But God heard the cry of my heart. Now, I want to share with you how I got where I am today and the journey that God has and still is taking me through to see His miracle power released in the earth.

I was born into a Christian family. I can't remember a day when I was a child that I didn't love the Lord. I had many encounters with the Lord throughout my childhood. In fact, when I was two-years-old, Jesus came into my room—this is actually a funny story. It all started when a rooster pecked at my finger. I was traumatized by the event and every night I would lay in my bed and cry because I was afraid that the roosters would come in my window and peck me.

One night, my parents decided I just needed to get over it, so they let me cry. As I was lying in bed crying alone, Jesus walked into my room. He sat on my bed and said, "It's okay you don't have to cry, I will watch over your window all night." Jesus spoke in a very simple and loving language that I understood. From that time on, I have always loved Him.

As early as I can remember, I always had a desire to serve the Lord. When I was really little, I would line up all of my stuffed animals and preach to them. When I was seven-years-old, my parents got divorced. It was a huge shock. The time was very devastating and difficult because I didn't see it coming. I remember so clearly the day my dad left. I was just sobbing in my bed and was very afraid, wondering who was going to be my dad? At that time of grief and pain, I have such a clear memory of the Lord's Presence coming into my room. He said, "Don't worry, I will be your Dad."

GOD'S PROVISION

My mom raised us to believe that God was our Father and that anything we needed, God would be the One to provide for us. We would pray when our cupboards were empty, and we would ask our Father for food. Every time we would get home from school, bags of groceries would be on our doorstep. We would never know who left them. We never missed a meal and God always provided.

I can remember another time I learned about faith from my mom. My brother ruined his only pair of shoes. We had no money, but Mom took us down to the shoe store and told my brother to go in and pick out his favorite pair of shoes. After he had picked out the shoes, Mom handed them to the salesman and asked, "How much are these shoes?" He told her $38.19. She said, "Thank you, we will be back." So we went home and just prayed and asked God for them.

The next day, we went to church and a lady came running up to my mom and said, "Please don't be offended by this, but God has been telling me that I have to give you $38.19." She took out her checkbook and wrote out a check for the exact amount that we needed for my brother's shoes. We were so touched by God that we went right to the store after church was over and bought the shoes that God had provided for my brother. All these experiences built my ability to trust in the Lord.

As I got into my early teens, a lot of my anger and pain that I had shoved down for so many years started coming to the surface. I call this my "dark era" because these were some very hard years. Although I was really hurting and broken, I still truly wanted to serve the Lord, but God felt a million miles away. People would continually give me prophecies about God's plans for my life, but I was a total mess. I was making terrible choices, and yet at the same time I was crying out to God saying, "I want to live for you!" Still, I was totally living for myself. This lasted for a couple of years. I am so grateful for the mercy of God during this time in my life and for the things He protected me from.

A Challenge from the Lord

When I was 16-years-old, I was sitting in Taco Bell with some friends, and God started to talk to me in the most profound way. I began to have a revelation of truth. God began to speak with me and He said, "Make a decision, I have had grace on your life, but the grace is getting ready to end. You are either for Me, or against Me. There is no more middle ground." He said, "What will it be? Are you going to serve Me, or are you going to serve yourself?"

At this time I didn't know any other teenagers that were passionately going after God. There wasn't a big movement of youth around in our area and the kids I knew in church were totally lukewarm. I had always heard, "Serve God or serve the devil," but never did I realize that I couldn't serve God and myself. Even though I didn't have a model of what this type of commitment looked like, I understood what this was going to cost me.

I remember going home and just mourning. Finally I said, "Okay God I am going to serve you with my whole heart!" I exchange "my will" for "Your will." I thought to myself, well now that I have made this commitment to the Lord my life is going to be so exciting. But it wasn't exciting at all. It was so difficult. During the last two years of high school, the Lord asked me to lay down all my friends that were bad influences, so I laid my friends down.

SURRENDERING ALL

The University of Southern California was my dream school. I had worked hard to get there and I had even received a scholarship. The Lord spoke to me the night before I was leaving for school and said to me, "I will bless you if you go, but this isn't my highest will for you. Will you lay this down?"

This was like a stab in my back. I had worked my hardest for four years to get accepted there. My family didn't like the idea of me not going, but I said, "Okay, Lord, I will lay this down." I did what the Lord asked me to do and went to another university instead. Although this was a very difficult time for me, it was a real season of growth as the Lord purified and healed me. I worked two jobs and took twice as many classes in school as I was supposed to.

I had thought that laying down everything to follow Jesus was an invitation to travel the world and have great adventures, that my life was going to be easy, but it wasn't. Yet, during this time my heart was filled with visions, dreams and prophetic encounters, but I had no outlets. The Lord kept asking me, "Will you continue to trust me? Will you continue to love me?"

At 19-years-old, I got into a very serious relationship with a young man and wanted to get married. I needed to hear from the Lord on this relationship. Was this really His perfect will for my life? This was another one of the huge circumstances that God used to give me an opportunity to give up my own will. I asked Him what His will was and He gave me a choice. He said, "If you want to marry this person, I will bless it, it will be my permissive will, but this isn't my highest will for you. Will you lay this down?"

This was such a difficult decision for me because it was the only thing left that I wanted to hold onto in my life. Somehow I felt that if God took away this deepest desire of my heart, it would not be consistent with His character. But then I realized that every time I gave up something, I had the biggest breakthrough of my life and would feel His Presence in a greater way than ever before. I laid down the relationship. I entered a season of grieving and healing as God healed me from this relationship.

The Beginning of an Adventure

When I graduated from college, I felt pretty dead to myself. The good news is that I was feeling very alive in my spirit. I jokingly said to God, "I don't think there is anything else to die to—I have died to everything." Then the Lord said, "I want you to move to Canada." Sure enough, there was still one more thing for me to die to. By then I had learned to just give in because God always knows best. I left everything—my apartment, my car, and my life—and I moved to Canada. I thought, "What am I doing here? What is this all about?"

Shortly after this, God said, "Ralph Bromley is going to offer you something, and whatever he offers you, you are going to accept." Ralph Bromley was the man I was staying with in Canada who is one of my greatest mentors and a father in the Lord. This wasn't an audible voice of God, but it was a knowing in my heart. One day Ralph came to me and said, "I think you're supposed to go to Africa. Go for six months by yourself."

I thought, you have to be kidding me, but I agreed and said, "Okay God." As I went through the process of dying to myself, I felt like I had been in a huge motion of going downward. Every time I said, "Yes," to the Lord, I felt like He was taking me lower and lower. Yet, every time the Lord would walk me through another death, I would receive greater life from the Spirit.

It was then that I remembered what the Lord had spoken clearly to me on June 5, 2001, when I had just graduated from college before I had even gone to Canada. I was 21, I had given up everything, and I had just been crying out to the Lord about all of my frustrations, telling Him how I wanted to get married. He said, "I want to send you on a great mission, and it is going to cost you absolutely everything. It's going to be very difficult. It's going to be very lonely, the loneliest time you will ever walk through. It will be painful, it will be hard, and the only thing familiar to you will be My Presence. I want you to betroth yourself to Me the way you would marry a natural husband. I want you to give Me all of your time, your will, and your emotions."

This wasn't the news I had wanted to hear at that point. I had no clue what the Lord was talking about. He said, "If you accept this mission, this is about gaining authority, this is about spiritual promotion. Will you commit to doing this for a year?" To me a whole year seemed like an eternity. Would it be a year of hell? Finally I said, "Okay." Then the Lord asked, "Will you commit two years?"

I just broke down and cried and cried. How do I say no to the Lord? So I responded, "Okay, Lord, I will commit for two years." Then He said, "Will you commit for three years?" That was so difficult that I felt like the knife couldn't be any deeper in my heart.

When I was 16, I had made a vow before the Lord that I would never say no to Him. I answered, "Okay, whatever you want to do Lord. I am yours." Little did I know that the life of adventure that I thought I was going to have years before when I exchanged my will for His was about to begin in Africa.

My Arrival in Africa

I arrived in northern Kenya and there I came in contact with an African tribe called the Turkana tribe. They were very primitive, half dressed with rings up to their necks, like something straight out of National Geographic. The situation there was unbearable. It was 120 degrees every day with sand as far as the eye could see and not a tree in sight. There was no life—everything was brown. There was no water and people were dying.

Adults and even children would literally throw themselves in front of our vehicle. It was either hit them or stop. When we stopped, they would just beg you to put one drop of water on their tongue. The children's hands were bloody from digging for water for hours and days in the sand before they would die. There was massive famine and the animals were skinny and withering away. The only reason these people were even alive was because World Vision was there dishing out food.

In addition to all this, it was incredibly violent there. People were being murdered every day in tribal wars. If you were white, you were a huge target. Not only was I white, the men in the Turkana tribe didn't like women—and there I was, alone, a single young white woman who had just come from America. Beyond this I had come to this desert region of Kenya to help women and children by starting a women's organization for Ralph Bromley's ministry, Hope for the Nations.

In order to get into a village, I had to be escorted by guards with AK-47s who hung out the window to protect us from those trying to open fire on our vehicle. To make conditions even worse, the day I arrived I received a notice from an organization that was sending money for the mission saying they were unable to give us the grant. I had just arrived in Africa and I was supposed to stay for six months. Now I was stuck out in the middle of nowhere, the mission I had come to establish was not going to be funded, and there was no one to help me.

A New Challenge

Just when I was certain that things couldn't get any worse, I found out that the Turkana tribe had made blood covenants with Satan which were thousands of years old, dating back to the foundation of their tribe. There were so many curses and demonic strongholds in this land that all the people were just living cursed lives. The drought and the famine were all part of the curse.

Because I am not a superstitious person, I had to decide what was real and what was just silly superstition. What I found out was—it was all real. If these people didn't pay homage to the demons by blood sacrifice, their family and all their livestock would bleed though their nose until they died. If the sacrifice they made was not the right sacrifice, their huts and everything in them would just blow up. Consequently, the people lived in terrible fear, and they were very careful to appease these demons.

The Christians in this land were under the same curse. Some of the pastors there came up to me and asked, "What's the deal? We love God, but a curse was put on us that every one of our newborn babies would die within 24 hours. We thought, well we are Christians and it can't happen to us, but sure enough every one of our babies has died within 24-hours of birth."

I had no answers for them. I had thought being a Christian was enough. I found myself in a situation where I felt very small, and everything I was facing seemed so huge. I thought, what in the world can I do? "God," I cried, "You picked the wrong person for this job. I don't know how to break a thousand years of blood covenants. I am so inadequate." I had such compassion for these people, but I thought, "What can one person do?"

Then the Lord spoke to me, "You are totally and completely inadequate, and don't ever forget it. It's your greatest strength. Are you willing to rely on Me for a strategy? Do you still believe that I use Davids to take down Goliaths?" Hope came into my heart and I thought, maybe God really could use a little nobody to do something about this.

My first response was in human wisdom. I emailed my mentor telling him some of my ideas. He said, "Those are all great ideas, but go back and get God's strategy." A month before this God had spoken to me that a minister needed to be there whom I had met in Argentina about three years before named Arthur Burke.

Arthur does things with communities to break curses, but to get him to come to Kenya seemed impossible because he didn't even know who I was. I had no money to pay for him to come. Nevertheless, I sent him an email telling him the situation and asking if he would come out and help us? He emailed us back and said that God told him to change his schedule and cancel everything and come. He said the only way that these people could get out of the blood covenant was to enter into a stronger covenant.

Some of our local people and I got on our faces before the Lord, and God began to give us an idea. We were to call all the leaders from the region to come together to a conference. Because it was the founding leaders that established this blood covenant with Satan, all the leaders of this generation would have to break it. We thought this was a start.

A Willingness to Sacrifice My Life

After this, the Lord said, "I am so proud of you, but I want you to know that if you go through with this, Satan will try to kill you." I had to ask myself, am I willing to lay my life down for a whole people group to get saved. This was easy for me because I had already given up my life. I said, "Yes, Lord, I am willing, but I know that Satan can't do anything to me that You don't permit because my life is in Your hands."

Within 24 hours after God told me this, there was such a demonic attack against me that I became terribly ill. I got worse and worse, and got to a point where I couldn't move. This poor guy Arthur who came out to speak had to take care of me. I knew that if God didn't show up I was going to die. I cried out to the Lord and He sent me help.

A guy named Randy Coates who lived 14 hours away was out exploring and happened to drop by. When he saw my condition, he drove me back 14 hours to the hospital. The doctors said that had I arrived two hours later I would have died. They were not sure even then that I would live. So there I was at the hospital, totally alone and dying on Christmas day.

I went to sleep and had an encounter with the Lord. In the middle of the encounter I woke up and God told me to go over to the window and look out. I looked and saw one million soldiers standing at attention in perfect formation outside my hospital window. As I was trying to figure out what they were doing there, God said, "See, you're not alone. You have no idea how many angels I have standing at attention looking out for you. You are not alone."

That did it for me. When I woke up, the Christians who were looking after me came with a prophetic word saying that this whole ordeal was about spiritual promotion. The doctors, however, had no idea what was wrong with me and still told me that I was going to die. When the doctors made that statement, I became very mad at the devil. Something rose up inside of me and I began fighting for my life.

After this, I was asleep one day in the hospital, and Jesus walked into my room. He took the side of his hand, cut me open, cleaned up each organ in my body one by one, and then closed up my skin. He had my skin color in his hand and colored in the scar. I woke up and I didn't feel any better, in fact I felt awful. Nevertheless, I started to yell, "I am healed! I am healed!"

Everyone thought that I was going crazy, but every time I yelled, "I am healed!" I felt strength come into me. Then I said, "I am hungry, bring me food." I hadn't eaten in 10 days. I ate tons of food. The doctors sent me for eight hours of testing, and the same doctors that said I was going to die came back and confirmed that

I was healed! I knew God could do miracles, but now I had entered into a whole new level of authority in His miracle working power.

GOD'S PROTECTION

I left the hospital and was recovering in the guesthouse where I was staying. One night, I heard five guys talking. I heard the voice of the devil say, "I told you that I am going to destroy you. I have sent five men to rape and kill you." Suddenly, these men started to break into my little house. I was stricken with fear.

The Lord said to me, "Hurry up and decide if you are going to react with fear or faith? Your life depends on it." I responded, "God, I have no idea how you are going to get me out of this, but I choose faith." Immediately, all these Bible verses started coming back to me. As I started quoting them, faith started to flood my heart. Fear completely left my body—I was so consumed with faith that I jumped out of bed. At that point, I completely understood who I was as God's child. I was one hundred percent convinced that if these men stepped foot in my room that God would strike them dead. There was no doubt in my mind. I actually felt sorry for them.

I rushed to a window and saw three men at the window and two at the door. As I was walking, I slipped on a plastic bag on the floor and fell back unconscious, but God was in charge. He said, "I'll take care of this." The noise of my fall freaked the men out. Motion lights were set off and the dog started barking. They were all afraid and ran off. I believe that if I would have chose fear instead of faith, it would have been an open door for the enemy to come in.

BREAKING THE CURSE

After my recovery, I returned to the village. Runners were sent out to each village to summon all the political, ministry, and tribal leaders to come for a meeting to break the ancient covenants that had been made with Satan. Many had to walk for days to attend this meeting, yet 1,500 leaders showed up from the villages. We told them what they needed to do in order for all these curses to be broken and for the blessing of God to return to the land.

The people were freaked out because this was so serious. If God wasn't in this thing, everyone would die. We were in the peak of the drought and the high point of the demonic activity at a time when everyone was supposed to go to the middle of the desert to make their blood covenants. This was called the Appeasement of the Dead Ceremony, and anyone who didn't make the sacrifice would suffer. People were slaughtering tons of animals and doing demonic things everywhere to reinforce their covenant for the next year.

It was imperative that we listen to the Holy Spirit and obey. I had such a fear of God. I knew if we didn't listen to God and instead did things our way, this wouldn't work and it would cost many lives. So, we carefully did everything the Lord told us to do. We took communion and then we poured communion over the land and called it into covenant with the Lord Jesus Christ. The whole thing was very simple, but completely led by the Holy Spirit.

After we had done everything the Lord told us to do, we asked for two signs to know that He was pleased. We prayed, "Lord, will you give us a sign to show us that you have brought down this demonic covenant?" He gave us two signs. The heaven began to grow dark and it poured down rain—and this was a place where it doesn't rain. I felt like we were in a Bible story. This was our first sign.

Then suddenly, the second sign came. A bolt of lighting came out of the sky and struck "Goat Mountain," a mountain where the witchdoctors gathered and people from all over the world came to see them. The witchdoctors were all up on Goat Mountain offering their sacrifices when the lightning bolt hit.

Instantly their demonic power dried up. They broke out in terrible fear and came running down the mountain thinking that they were going to be killed. Seeing that the witchdoctors were running down the mountain, the youth who had gathered together with the leaders to break the satanic covenants left the conference, ran to the bottom of the mountain, and waited for the witchdoctors to talk to them about the Lord. /

Immediately, I began winning more people in the tribe to the Lord. One witchdoctor went through three months of non-stop deliverance, manifesting for three months until every demon was out of him. This guy became a big key to intersession for the place. These signs and wonders were awesome, but I still wasn't satisfied. Signs and wonders are great, but they are not an end in themselves. It wasn't enough for me. I wanted to see people's lives really changed.

On the last day of the conference, my friends, the young couple who were pastors whose babies died when the land was under the curse, delivered a perfect baby girl. The pastor held his baby up in front of the conference and named her Peace, saying she would be a prophetic example to everyone. When they saw her, they would remember that the day she was born was the day they came into peace with the Living God. This was the beginning of getting rid of poverty and the adverse effects of the curses that had been on the land.

EXPANDING HIS KINGDOM

When I went back to the region eight months later, there was grass everywhere there had been sand. The climate had changed and the extreme temperatures had decreased. The animals were fat. World Vision moved out because the people and land were doing so well. There hadn't been one murder in eight months. I didn't need any armed guards to take me in. This whole experience transformed me—the God of the Bible is still the God of today.

At this time I began working with some orphans. God told me to start with these little straggly street children. I sat in the dirt with these children everyday and tried to teach them an undiluted Gospel straight from the Bible. Everything I said to them they just believed.

When I told them a story of healing, I would say, "Go and heal the sick!" They would say, "Okay," and then they would go pray for the sick. This command was straight from the Word. The children would go right into hospitals or wherever the sick were, and the sick would be healed. This began a movement of children. It started with a few kids. These few kids soon became 10 kids, then 50, 100, 600, 5000 kids who got it. Children began to walk with God and began to understand the Creator and have His authority.

My ministry, now called the "Global Children's Movement,"[1] grew out of this movement of God's Spirit among the children in Africa. It all started with sitting in the dirt with a few kids just obeying what God asked me to do. We have been training kids and youth in several countries as well as training leaders how to strategically mentor them. My main message is that God still uses Davids to take out Goliaths. This is what God had me first walk out through my own life experiences. We have kids that take out massive Goliaths in their communities. Kids will even use prayer to change unjust laws in the government. They will pray and fast until that law is changed.

The whole journey that God walked me through was preparation for my message to this generation. The message is that we are inadequate, and the moment that you think you have it all together, you have just disqualified yourself. God is looking for humble, simple, obedient people. He is not concerned with what you know, how many great programs you have been too, or anything else. He is still looking for the humble person who can just say, "I don't know what I am doing, but here am I, choosing to step out and obey You in full surrender." This is the Gospel of the Kingdom.

This is what we live by. We make the Gospel simple. We don't take any projects on that we can do in our own strength. Why should we do what has already been done? We need to get out of the way so God can show up. We need to raise the bar for what we believe. This generation is called to do so much more than the generations in the past.

By the way, after my three-year commitment with God, I got married the very next day. God divinely worked it out and gave me my original heart's desire and so much more. I want to see this next generation really get it and give their lives for His service and not care about building up a great name for themselves.

My prayer for you is that the Word of God would become alive in your spirit and that you would truly know who you are in Him. In that place, you will be given an authority that will release you to a place of power as a child of the Kingdom.

ಬಾ☙⚜❧ಚೃ

Jennifer's ministry grew from a dream she had in her heart as a little girl. Although the seeds of her dream lay dormant for many years, when the time was right the Spirit of God began to move in Jennifer's heart to bring her to a place of total surrender so that dream could become a reality.

All those who desire to be used by God will be led to this place of full surrender. One by one we will each be brought to the place of choosing and there will not be many choices, just two—God's will and an alternative.

chapter 3

WHEN NO ONE SEES

Nothing happens unless first we dream.

—CARL SANDBURG (1878-1967)

WINNER OF THE PULITZER PRIZE FOR HIS
BIOGRAPHY OF ABRAHAM LINCOLN

If you listen to your fears, you will die without knowing
what a great person you might have been.

—DR. ROBERT SCHULLER

PASTOR OF THE CRYSTAL CATHEDRAL, AUTHOR, AND
MEMBER OF THE ACADEMY OF ACHIEVEMENT

Don't underestimate the value of Doing Nothing,
Of just going along, listening to all the things
You can't hear, and not bothering.

—WINNIE THE POOH

A.A. MILNE

In the beginning, God was the Prevailing Presence—the Imagina-
tive Power— hovering, brooding over the earth, looking to create
something. And He still is. The Bible tells us that "The eyes of the

Lord are moving to and from throughout the whole earth that He may strongly support those whose hearts are completely His"(2 Chron. 16:9 NAS).

Is your heart completely His? If it is, then you are the one He is looking for. He wants to strongly support you. He wants to continue His creation through you. He invites you to be a co-creator with Him to the end that "His kingdom will come" and His "will shall be done on earth as it is in heaven." For this, He told us to pray.

To be an instrument that God can use, you need to recognize the importance of the dream. To be a co-creator with God, His dreams must find a place to lodge in your heart—and they must be fed by your imagination. To understand more about a God-dream, let's look at the story of one the Bible's greatest dreamers.

One night Joseph had a dream and promptly reported the details to his brothers, causing them to hate him even more. "Listen to this dream," he announced. "We were out in the field tying up bundles of grain. My bundle stood up and then all your bundles gathered around and bowed low before it."

"So you are going to be our king are you," his brothers taunted him. And they hated him all the more for his dream and for what he had said.

Then Joseph had another dream and told his brothers about it. "Listen to this dream. The sun, moon, and eleven stars bowed down before me."

This time he told his father as well as his brothers; and his father rebuked him. "What do you mean?" his father asked. "Will your mother, your brothers, and I actually come to bow before you?" But while his brothers were jealous of Joseph, his father gave it some thought and wondered what it all meant (Gen. 27:5-11, NLT).

Maybe you've had an experience like Joseph. You have been captivated by a dream. You have shared the dreams God has given you with others, and they have discouraged you. The tragedy is that many people let the discouraging words of others become the graveyard of their dreams. They decide to forget their dreams and reason, "I was full of pride to think that I was that special."

Self-exaltation is what we usually think of when we think of pride. However, there is another form of pride that is rooted in the desire for man's approval. The highest form of pride is the idolatry of self that loves the praises of men more than the praises of God. We participate in this idolatry when we try to make our dreams fit into the very small box of what everyone else does in order to gain the approval of others.

Joseph could have done that. He could have made a confession to the sin of pride, renounced his God-dreams, and he might have continued to live happily in the fellowship of his brothers. But the source of Joseph's dreams wasn't a desire for self-exaltation. God was the author of his dreams.

If Joseph had decided to apologize for his dreams and submit to the opinions of men, he may have never made it to Egypt because his brothers may not have thrown him into the pit and sold him as a slave. His desire for his brothers' approval more than for the fulfillment of the will of God could have kept him out of God's purpose. God in turn used the jealousy and wrath of Joseph's brothers to fulfill His intentions.

THE DANGER OF BEING A MAN-PLEASER

The Bible records the very real possibility that being a man-pleaser can shut you out of the purposes of God. Saul's continual disobedience to God because he was afraid that he would lose the approval of men cost him his kingdom. Finally, God told Samuel, "I am sorry that I ever made Saul king, for *he has not been loyal to Me* and has again refused to obey me"(1 Sam.15:10-11 NLT). If you read Saul's story, you will notice that he was always concerned about the opinions of men. God called this disloyalty. His final act of disobedience was in his battle with the Amalekites.

The Lord told Saul to kill all the people and animals and leave nothing alive, yet Saul allowed the men to save the best sheep from slaughter and to spare the king. Because the customary payment for soldiers was the spoils of war, Saul was probably afraid that if he did not let his men take something from the battle they would be angry with him. On the way home from the battle the Bible tells us that Saul "set up a monument to himself" (1 Sam. 15:12).

When Samuel met Saul coming from battle and asked him why he had disobeyed God, Saul kept insisting that he had obeyed God and had killed the Amalekites. Samuel asked, "What then is this bleating of the sheep in my ears, and the lowing of the oxen which I hear?" Saul explained that he had carried out God's orders and had killed men, women, children, and animals, but he had saved the best sheep to sacrifice them to the Lord.

God didn't give Saul a pass and say, "Well he did most of what I said." God didn't grade Saul on a curve; He called Saul's ninety-eight percent obedience, disobedience. Samuel answered, "What is more pleasing to the Lord: your burnt offerings and sacrifices or your obedience to His voice? Obedience is far better than sacrifice. Listening to Him is much better than offering the fat of rams. Rebellion is as bad as the sin of witchcraft, and stubbornness is as bad as worshiping idols. So because you have rejected the word of the Lord, He has rejected you from being king" (1 Sam.15:10-11, 22 NLT).

The temptation to seek the praises of men above the will of God is a test that each of us must encounter one day because, if we follow on to know the Lord, we will be persecuted by others. Persecution is not a bad thing. In fact, it is a great sign that you are doing the works of God.

Jesus reminds us, "If they persecuted Me, they will persecute you" (John 15:20). "Blessed are those who are persecuted for righteousness sake for theirs is the kingdom of heaven. Blessed are you when men revile you and persecute you and say all kinds of evil against you falsely for My sake. Rejoice and be exceedingly glad, for great is your reward in heaven for so they persecuted the prophets who were before you" (Matt. 5:10-12). Paul reminds us, "Everyone who wants to live a godly life in Christ Jesus will suffer persecution"(2 Tim. 3:12 NLT).

If you yield to the temptation to seek man's approval instead of the will of God, this will cause you to walk in unbelief, which will ultimately lead to disobedience. We must take Jesus' admonition to heart: "How can you believe, who receive honor from one another, and do not seek the honor that comes from the only God?" (John 5:44) According to Jesus, we can't even *believe* if we are seeking the praises of men. God wants you to look into His eyes, see what He has created you to be, and seek His approval and not man's. Once you are certain the dream in your heart is from God, make sure you don't let it go, regardless of what anyone says.

THE IMPOSSIBLE DREAM

Before Joseph could see his dream fulfilled, he had to go through a few delays along the way—and so will everyone who follows the Lord. If he had looked only at his circumstances, he would have thought his dream was impossible. But God was using all his circumstances as his training ground. Although a slave in Potiphar's house, Joseph was set over the whole household where God taught Joseph to serve and to run his master's affairs. God tested his integrity when Potiphar's wife tried to seduce him. Regardless of his faithful and loyal service, Joseph was falsely accused and thrown in jail. Here, Joseph had favor with all the guards and with the prisoners as he managed and ran the whole prison.

The first place we hear of Joseph interpreting dreams is in jail. No one trained him to do this, but God Himself trained Joseph even in these impossible conditions. He could have become bitter, hardhearted, and believed that God had forsaken him, when the truth was that God was preparing him to manage the entire kingdom of Egypt and setting him up to speak to Pharaoh. Unknown to Joseph, prison would become his launching pad to catapult him into being second in command in all of Egypt.

Never underestimate or be discouraged by the circumstances you are in right now. If you trust in the Lord, He will use your circumstances to prepare you for His purposes. Your circumstances are your opportunity to learn to look to God and see His miraculous power in the face of adversity and impossibility. When Joseph was placed as second in command in Egypt, how could Joseph have ever taken the glory for himself and thought that there was something great in himself that caused him to earn such a position?

SELF-EFFORT, A WORK OF THE FLESH

When delay looks you in the face and mocks your dream, impatience can push you to work in your own strength to bring the vision to pass. Remember the trial of Abraham, who is the father of faith to all those who believe. God took 25 years to fulfill His promise to Abraham and send the promised son. Abraham got discouraged halfway through the trial, took Sarah's advice, and tried to help God out. He wound up with Ishmael, called by Paul "a child of the flesh."

What is the flesh? Oswald Chambers has described the "flesh" as "self-effort of every kind." And Paul reminds us, "Those who are in the flesh cannot please God" (Rom. 8:8). Paul told the Galatians that Ishmael represents the child of the flesh and was born "in a human attempt to bring about the fulfillment of God's promise." But Isaac was born "as God's own fulfillment of His promise" (Gal. 4:23 NLT). God told Abraham, "At the appointed time I will return to you…and Sarah shall have a son" (Gen. 18:14). As a result of a visitation from God, Isaac was born.

God waited to bring Isaac into the picture when it was beyond all human possibility for Sarah to have a child. This way there could be no doubt about who was responsible for this miracle. This resulted in all praise to God. Here we find the mark of a God given dream appearing—impossible with man, possible with God.

If it is possible to fulfill the dream in your own strength, then the dream isn't from God. Through all your striving and self-effort, you will be able to do it. This does not develop your trust in God because you never step out of your own ability and have no need to trust Him. You can go ahead and pride yourself in your accomplishment, and take the glory for yourself—all credit goes to your ability.

Not only can self-effort never bring forth the work of the Spirit, you will be totally frustrated if you try to bring forth the works of God's Spirit. Those involved in the strife of self-effort often become persecutors of those who are bringing forth the true works of God.

Paul reminds us, "Just as Ishmael, the child of ordinary birth, born according to the flesh despised and persecuted him who was born remarkably according to the promise and the working of the Holy Spirit, so it is now" (Gal.4:29 AMP). It is not by doing things our own way that the dreams of God are fulfilled, but it is by believing that what God has promised, He will bring to pass, as we spend time in His Presence, listen to His instructions, and obey His Spirit.

Entering God's Rest

The dream of the Promised Land was postponed for 40 years because the Israelites doubted themselves more than they trusted God. Israel's sins of disobedience and unbelief resulted in self-will and self-effort and kept Israel out of the Promised Land, leaving them to wander in the wilderness. About them God said, "Their hearts always turn away from Me. They refuse to do what I tell them…They will never enter My place of rest" (Heb. 3:10-11 NLT).

The New Testament writer reminds us, "God's promise of entering His place of rest still stands, so we ought to tremble with fear that some of you might fail to get there. For this Good News—that God has prepared a place of rest—has been announced to us just as it was to them. But it did them no good because they didn't believe what God told them. For only we who believe can enter His place of rest" (Heb. 4:1-3 NLT).

We enter into His rest when the power is "of God and not of ourselves"(2 Cor. 4:7b NAS). And believing is not a hard thing. It is as simple as receiving God's word as truth and making up your mind that God doesn't lie.

Jesus' disciples asked Him, "What shall we do, that we may work the works of God?" Jesus answered, "This is the work of God, that you *believe in Him* whom He sent" (John 6:28-29). If we give up our desire for the praises of men and live for God's glory alone—if we give up all our attempts to produce the promises of God and let our thoughts rest in God's promises and His power to fulfill His own word—if we like Abraham and Joseph trust and believe in God, we will begin to realize our God-given dreams.

Paul reminds us, "Abraham believed God, so God declared him righteous because of his faith. The real children of Abraham are all those who put their faith in God" (Gal. 3:6-7 NAS). As we abandon unbelief and self-will, meditate in His word day and night, listen to the still small voice of His Spirit, then God will fill our minds with His highest thoughts and bring us into His highest purposes. Rest in His love—rely on Him.

David's advice comes down to us through the ages, "Trust in the Lord and do good...delight yourself also in the Lord and *He will give you the desires of your heart.* Commit your way to the Lord. Trust also in Him, and *He shall bring it to pass*" (Ps. 37:3-5 NAS).

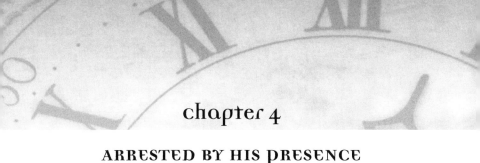

chapter 4

ARRESTED BY HIS PRESENCE

Let us lie low in the Lord's power and learn
that truth alone makes rich and great.

—EMERSON

SPIRITUAL LAWS

Derek Schneider was brought up in the church. His parents are pastors, and he always went to church and felt he was a Christian. One day he met Jesus face to face in an encounter that changed his life forever. He was arrested by God's Presence for God's purposes.

DEREK'S STORY

My mother was told by doctors that she would never bear children. Regardless of this bad report, my mother was a woman of faith, and like Hannah, she believed God to do the impossible. Along with Hannah she prayed, "O Lord Almighty, if you will look down upon my sorrow and answer my prayer and give me a son, then I will give him back to you. He will be yours for his entire lifetime" (1 Sam. 1:11). Like Hannah, God answered her prayer.

I was born in 1981, and am currently living in Oshawa, Ontario, Canada. I pray that my story will give glory to God and also inspire and spark faith in every person in the pursuit of his or her destiny in Christ.

As a young boy, I can remember hearing the voice of God, and though I didn't know Him well, I somehow sensed that God wanted to use me and do something with my life. As I grew up, the voice of God seemed to slowly become more and more unclear as I engaged in some of the typical attractions that this world is more than willing to offer a young person. I didn't ever completely turn my back on my faith in God, but many other desires began to slowly take first place in my life. The path of worldliness is truly a slippery slope, but praise God for His mercy and everlasting grace. It is amazing!

THE MUSIC THING

As I grew up, I had a love and passion for music (specifically hip-hop music) that eventually led me to perform in many small venues throughout the Greater Toronto area, and I loved every minute of it. I began to build a career in the music business, and though many of the lyrics in my songs were about God, my heart still did not fully know Him. As I look back on it now, I can see the hand of God on my life, even then, guiding me and blessing me in every way.

I had just completed high school when my career in hip-hop music really began to take off. I was being featured in magazines, small television shows, and on many major radio stations in the Toronto area. I began traveling and opened for Slim Shady. Things were going very smoothly for me, but strangely enough, at times I would feel a sense of dissatisfaction with my life and even slight depression.

I found that even as I pursued my passion, set goals for my career, and achieved them, I would end up feeling worse than before. I felt that my value as a person was dependent upon my career achievements. I was living what I thought was my dream, but

I was about to discover that outside the will of God, one will never experience true fulfillment.

I vividly remember when I found out that a small record label was interested in signing me to a three-year recording contract. I felt this was exactly what I needed and that I would really be happy once I had secured a real record deal. However God's timing is perfect, and before the label got the contract in my hands, I took a short vacation that would change my life forever.

THE POINT OF NO-RETURN

My family frequently took vacations at a beautiful place called Kelowna, British Columbia. We had relatives there, and it was the ideal setting for me to slow down, as the fast paced life of building a music career was taking its toll on my desire for a relationship with God. It is true that we can miss the voice of God in the busyness and hustle and bustle of life. It is those who understand how to quiet themselves before the Lord, very much like Samuel did, who will hear the word of the Lord for their lives, and for the lives of this generation.

Unfortunately, I was finding myself unable to enjoy my vacation. Something was stirring inside of me. God was allowing me to experience tension and unrest in my soul. I felt like I didn't know what my purpose was in life. I didn't know who I was anymore, and that's just what God wanted. One night, those feelings of confusion reached an all-time high, and I couldn't take it anymore. I felt as though all the money and fame in the world wouldn't satisfy me. I felt as though there was something missing in my life.

I knew who Jesus Christ was and had received Him into my heart at a young age, but I just couldn't figure out what was going on with me. The truth of the matter was, I was running from my calling and my true destiny. I was running from the very reason I was given life—to preach the Gospel and shine the light of Jesus Christ unashamedly in this generation.

On this particular night I had just come home from being out with some close family members. I did not let anyone know what was stirring inside of me. I remember retreating upstairs to the room where I was staying, planning to finally pray, and ask God what was going on.

I sat down in a chair in a corner of the room and just closed my eyes. I became so desperate for God that night that I responded to the drawing of His precious Holy Spirit and called out boldly, "Lord, I am just going to wait here in this chair, until You show up!" I can remember that I did not wait too long, until suddenly He was there. He was really there! I had never felt the Presence of the Lord like this ever in my life. It seemed as though the room became electric with His Presence.

I began to weep profusely and could feel Him all around me. It was unlike anything I had experienced before. To this day, I can't really say how long it lasted, but it seemed like hours—very wonderful hours. I remember flipping through the Bible and understanding things I had never understood before. I was reading scriptures that I had read or heard in church hundreds of times, but it seemed like I was hearing them for the first time. It was as if the Holy Spirit was giving me a personal tour of the scriptures.

I knew something was changing inside of me, and I felt as though my desire for a career in music was fading away in just those precious moments with the Lord. I felt as though I was about to lay down all I had for my desire to even just know God and fellowship with Him. A music career didn't seem to mean anything to me anymore.

Finally, at the climax of it all, I said to God, "What do I tell my manager and the label when I get back home?" I will never forget His answer. It is the meaning of life for the Christian and is what the world is waiting to see through us. He spoke it so clearly and powerfully, He said, "Tell them that you've seen my Face, and you'll never be the same!"

THE POWER OF HIS PRESENCE

I never was the same again after that night. I discovered that to see God's Face is to experience His Presence. To know Him, to really know Him, is our purpose. God will use those who are His—totally His. He will use those who desire Him more than a career, more than the things of this world, even more than ministry itself.

From that night onward I became hungry for the Lord. I craved those times alone with Him. I saw it as all that I needed. Little did I realize that in those hours spent with Him, He was training me and preparing me for ministry and doing a deep work in my heart so that I could be one of His vessels used for His service.

When I returned home from vacation, I did a few more concerts with my music that I had already committed myself to, but there was a definite change that had occurred. Strange things happened the last few times I performed. Once during the opening song, a demon possessed man began to manifest right there in front of the stage. A strange boldness came over me, and as I approached him he ran right out of the hall!

At another concert in a very worldly nightclub downtown, the place was packed with people, drugs and alcohol, and many corrupt things were taking place. I can remember praying backstage and asking the Holy Spirit to completely possess me. I told God that I didn't care about keeping a good reputation, or trying to impress people so that I could be successful. There were many important industry representatives watching me, yet all I wanted to do was preach Jesus!

After performing the third song, I couldn't take it anymore. I stopped the music and began preaching about the saving power of Jesus Christ. I waited for bottles or something to be thrown at me, but no bottles ever flew. It was a rough crowd, but for whatever reason they became totally silent as I briefly shared the Word of God. It was as though the Holy Spirit had taken over and everyone could only listen as their hearts were pricked. I figured if I was able to preach, then I might as well go ahead and give a quick altar call.

Up until then, nothing like this had ever taken place in a club like this, so I don't think the owners knew exactly how to handle it. It was an awesome opportunity and God knew what He was doing. I asked everyone who wanted to receive Jesus to raise their hands. Well let me tell you, hands went up all over that club and shortly thereafter, I was removed from the stage. Praise God! The Gospel is powerful, and the Holy Spirit will always back up His word.

After many more encounters and confirmations by the Lord, I left the music, my home, my immediate family, everything I knew, and moved out to Kelowna, British Columbia. I felt like Moses leaving Egypt and everything that was familiar to him to unknowingly enter God's training camp. I was determined to make it my mission to discover God in a deeper way. This was my next level of training, so I immediately enrolled in a small Bible school. I continued meeting with the Lord daily in that small bedroom in my grandparents' house where I had experienced my first encounter with Him that wonderful night.

To Preach the Gospel

I was living in Kelowna for a little more than a week when I received my first invitation to preach at a local youth church. For the life of me, I couldn't figure out why they would want me to preach. I had no reputation of being a preacher, and in fact, at that point I had never preached a real message in a church before. I found out later that the pastor there had heard of a few of my experiences in doing hip hop music and felt that I might have something to say to the young people. I was scared by this invitation and had partially turned it down, when I felt the Holy Spirit tug at my heart. I agreed to speak for him.

The day to preach finally arrived, and as nervous as I was, the Lord was faithful and moved powerfully that night. All glory to God! It was on this particular night that I felt what my heart had been longing for while building a music career. That empty void was satisfied as I preached about my one and only passion—Jesus! As I stood at that podium, I felt as though this was the reason I was alive. I felt that I had found something worth giving my life to—that I was beginning to fulfill a mission that had been handed to the people of the kingdom of God so long ago. It was a wonderful experience.

THE SOURCE OF THE ANOINTING

One of the amazing things about what God was doing in my life was that He was doing it fast. I didn't have to spend years locked away in a Bible college before I became "qualified" to minister. It seemed as though the only qualification I needed was that I walked closely with the Lord, and He with me. I truly loved Him, and out of that love relationship flowed true anointed ministry.

I believe that was the case in Jesus' day, and it still is today. Jesus released the disciples with such awesome power because they had spent time with Him. They had so yielded their lives to Him that God could trust them to be His vessels. I believe this is a truth that our generation is experiencing. It is not necessarily just about head knowledge, as important as knowledge is, but true spiritual life is this—to walk with God and allow Him to completely take your life unto Himself.

God definitely took my life and opened up doors left and right. I began to be asked to preach in many other churches in the area and was even able to perform my music as God permitted. It seemed as though God was using my reputation with my past music career to open up doors to preach. As my experiences with God in my quiet time grew, the level of His Presence seemed to grow in my ministry times.

I was once asked to perform my hip-hop music for about 200 young people at a Brethren Church youth group. That particular day, I had spent a long time with the Lord, and I remember having an overwhelming sense of His nearness to me. When I arrived at the church I felt His Presence become even greater until I felt myself begin to shake. As I walked up on stage I didn't perform any of my music, but I began to preach boldly.

As I spoke, I saw tears streaming down kids' faces as the wonderful Holy Spirit moved upon their hearts. The Glory of God was manifested so powerfully in that meeting that I did everything I could to hold myself together. It was heavenly. That night many wonderful things took place in that Brethren Church which they had never experienced before. Many who attended for the first time were wonderfully saved and signs and wonders were performed.

MORE OPEN DOORS

As God continued to train me, He entrusted me with more so that other ministry opportunities opened up by the grace of God. Many times I was able to profess Jesus on Kelowna's hottest local radio station, and I even performed at a crusade with 7,000 young people in attendance led by Miles McPherson (an evangelist from the United States).

Everywhere I went, my heart was always moved with compassion for the lost. Whether speaking publicly, or just walking down the street, or in a mall somewhere, I felt compelled to reveal the power of God everywhere. I can remember while being driven in the car, I would receive a prophetic word for someone who was walking down the street. My friends and I would stop the car, and I would jump out to speak with that person. We called them "prophetic drive-bys." We saw many come to the Lord that way.

I didn't realize that as you spend time with Jesus, you begin to become like Him. Jesus was a "radical"—in fact Jesus is a radical, and He loves being radical through us! Through all of these experiences, God was teaching me that one man, when yielded to God, can affect a church, a city, a nation, and even the world. I was young and "naïve," enough to really believe this—and God can use someone with a child-like faith.

Miracle Working Power

I praise God that He never gave up on me when I was living a life of compromise; God is so merciful and faithful. One of the things I believe that kept me from going completely off the deep end in my spiritually weaker days was that I came from a Christian home with a praying mother and father. In fact, my father was a minister and incredible role model for me.

When God began to use me, I would phone home from British Columbia to tell my parents all that God was doing. It wasn't long before my father invited me to travel with him to Europe to Amsterdam where he was scheduled to preach at a conference with a well-known man by the name of Sunday Adelaja. I did not realize at the time that, through this particular trip, God was going to change my life all over again.

Pastor Sunday Adelaja is the pastor of a 25,000-member church in Kiev, Ukraine and is being used mightily by the Lord to bring complete transformation to the Ukraine and beyond. He was scheduled to speak the first night of the conference in Amsterdam.

I sat up front with my father; eager to hear his message and experience his ministry.

One of the notable characteristics of Pastor Sunday's ministry is a real anointing in the area of physical healing. Up until this conference, I had only witnessed a few healings and even less through my ministry. I watched as the power of God moved through this man.

Nearing the close of his message, I was moved to tears. Again something was stirring inside me, my spirit was leaping, and I was hungry for more of God. I listened as many gave testimonies of the awesome miracles that God was performing at this conference. I wanted this miracle working power. I wanted to see greater miracles in North America. There was dissatisfaction again in my soul.

I have since learned that with God there is always more, always something greater in God. That first night of the conference I wanted the "greater." As Pastor Sunday finished speaking, I walked over to him and asked if he would pray for me. I told him that God is doing great things in North America, but I wanted to see more.

Before I had even finished speaking, he laid his hands on me almost violently and began to pray for me. To this day, I don't remember all that he said, but I remember my body shaking like I had never experienced before. Tears streamed down my face, and I was almost frightened by the power of God going through my body. Apparently the whole experience caused quite a commotion. My dad described it as the sound of two men fighting. I still laugh just thinking about it.

By the time that Pastor Sunday had finished praying for me, I had collapsed on the ground and felt as though there was an open door into heaven above me. I felt and heard many things, one of which was, "Derek, don't ever doubt me again—I'm going to use you!"

A NEW MOVE OF GOD

Shortly after this, I moved back home to Oshawa, Ontario, from Kelowna, B.C. and received a youth and young adults' pastoring position at my father's church. Little did I realize God was about to release something in the young people at our church that would have the potential to transform a city.

The youth and young adults' ministry at our church is called Fusion. Fusion had just come through a difficult season, which had caused its numbers to decrease drastically. Many had even turned their backs on God altogether. The spiritual climate at Fusion was low, but it was the perfect opportunity for God to do something fresh—and He was about to do it.

The first night I was scheduled to give leadership, there was a young lady with a kidney disease who had come to the service with her friend. She was in tremendous pain. I saw this as an opportunity for God to change the atmosphere at Fusion. I prayed for her, and she was healed by the power of Jesus! Praise God! The doctor confirmed the report the following week. At the same time, I noticed that the numbers had increased slightly in our attendance.

God continued to move in these meetings powerfully, and many more people were saved and healed almost weekly. Fusion began to grow at a phenomenal rate, from 10 to 20 people to 150 a night within just six months. The glory of God was incredible in our Friday night services, and people drove great distances to be a part of all that God was doing.

Many were being healed, delivered, and saved, and the testimonies of God's power continued and began to create "no small stir" in the area. One particular boy was healed of Turrets Syndrome, a terrible disorder that had kept him bound for most of his young life. We saw young people come in to church on crutches and leave walking in perfect condition. One woman took out her contact lenses and has had her sight increase to the point where she no longer needs to wear glasses or contacts. Often, people were healed as they left the service. Many young people who were addicted to cigarettes, after being prayed for, never had a craving again.

Services would sometimes go to one o'clock in the morning, as we would be filled with the joy of the Lord and dance in the Spirit. These services were so intense that we would try to have different events that would be geared more towards relationships and getting to know one another. The only problem was that these "socials" would quickly turn into Holy Spirit revival meetings.

One of our young people opened up his home for us to have a time of fellowship, and the Spirit of God broke out in an incredible way right in his home. A few of us were upstairs prophesying over people, and many were downstairs overcome by the power of God and were speaking in tongues. I can remember it sounding like hundreds of drunken people in the basement! The only thing I could compare it to was what it must have sounded like for the early church on the day of Pentecost.

What a wonderful God we serve! The faith level grew immensely in the young people's lives, and the fruit was very much evident. We heard reports of young people stirring up their high schools for Jesus with prophetic evangelism. One girl came home from a Friday night service shaking under the power of God.

When she woke up the next morning and went to work, she was still shaking. Her boss finally took her aside and questioned her because he thought that she was on drugs. She did her best to explain to him what was going on, and this testimony led to two people at her workplace giving their hearts to the Lord that very day. Others wanted to hear more about what God was doing. Many signs and wonders were taking place and have continued to this day.

I personally had a concern that if we just relied on great Friday night "Glory Services," we could lose some of those who were being saved and err in the area of true discipleship. It was the desire of my heart to raise up powerful young people who knew how to love the move of the Spirit, but also who were well versed in the richness of God's Word. We launched cell groups, which have been extremely crucial to the continued growth and discipleship of those who are being saved.

You can imagine the life that was all over. It not only had an effect on the adult community of our church, but it affected our city as well. The young people began to realize that God was moving in this way so that we could be a blessing to the city and to the churches of the region. Not only was a lot of evangelism going on in the community, but also ideas were being birthed on how to really get the city's attention and let them know that God was in our city, because we as believers were in the city.

A NEW CAMPAIGN

We organized a small campaign called, "God is in this City" and made many huge signs on white board with black lettering stating the same slogan. The Lord had spoken to me about the power of proclaiming the truth in our region, so we took the signs to the busiest intersections at the busiest times in the city and had many young people gathered around them.

The response was incredible and quickly became the talk of the city. Cars were stopping to ask why we were doing this, and many opportunities arose to witness. One Christian bus driver would pass one of the signs each day on his bus route and used it as a tool to speak to every person that got on his bus about Jesus. Praise the Lord! God was making His Presence known, and it had only just begun.

It's been a little over a year now since we put on that campaign, and God has not stopped moving. We have made arrangements to hold the "God is in this City" campaign again, only it will lead up to a city wide "Unity and Miracle Service" to be held at our local airport grounds.

We are inviting as many people as hear about it, and we have also invited other churches of many denominations to attend this one night service. The purpose of the event is to bring believers together in the Spirit of unity and to display that God is in our city through the demonstration of this powerful Gospel! We have invited young and old alike, but it will be solely a youth and young adult led event.

Through sponsoring this event, I have been able to meet with pastors all over the city. As a result, pastors are becoming aware of not only the importance of what God desires to do in the young people of this generation, but also understanding the need for the older generation to take on the role of spiritual mothers and fathers.

I believe that God is raising up young people who have been hand-picked and forged by the hand of God for ministry in all different types of capacities of training. I believe that this is a Samuel generation—a generation of young people who more than anything else desire the manifest Presence of God and are able to hear the word of the Lord in a season when the church needs it most. Young Samuel lay near the Ark and learned to hear the voice of God, and that same prophetic mantle is on this generation.

Since I received my first visitation from the Lord close to three years ago, He has continued to be merciful to me and use me, but He also has continued to train me. I have had the privilege of being in the presence of some great men and women of God.

God, in His wisdom, is releasing young people in extraordinary anointing with a covering of wonderful mentors and spiritual fathers and mothers. God has not neglected this generation's young people for a second—in fact, it is just the opposite. For some time now He has been forging them and preparing them—some even in their bedrooms, to usher in this next move of the Spirit in the world.

॰ॐ ॐ ॐ॰

After reading Derek's story, maybe you know that the Lord is calling you to be a part of the Samuel generation. Why not just bow your head and tell the Lord that you desire His Presence more than anything else. Ask Him to open your ears so that you can hear the voice of His Spirit and then—whatever He says to you—do it!

chapter 5

THE POWER OF KNOWING JESUS

When you aim for the stars, you get the stars,
but when you aim for the heavens, you get the stars thrown in.

—FROM THE LONDON PRODUCTION

OF *MARY POPPINS*

Seek first the kingdom of God and His righteousness,
and everything you need will be given to you.

—JESUS

MATTHEW 6:33

Although God created you with a special purpose in mind, you were created first of all for an intimate relationship with Him. Jesus proclaimed, "And this is eternal life, that they may know You, the only true God, and Jesus Christ whom He has sent" (John 17:3). Paul reminds us, "He is the one who invited you into this wonderful friendship with His Son, Jesus Christ our Lord" (1 Cor. 1:9 NLT). Through this friendship you become complete and the whole world stands open before you.

Would you ever construct a building without first consulting the architect and his blueprints? Of course not! Yet, people do this everyday. They go about their busy lives and want God to bless what they do, but they never take time to spend in fellowship with

Him, to love Him, and know Him, or to seek His will for their lives. As a result they never experience the great and wonderful blessings of His kingdom, His joy beyond measure, or fulfill the plans of the Great Architect of their soul.

BEING A DOER OF THE WORD

Jesus told His disciples what it would take to live in His Kingdom and why continuing in fellowship with Him was so important. "Not everyone who says to Me, 'Lord, Lord,' shall enter the kingdom of Heaven. Only those who actually do the will of my Father in heaven will enter. On judgment day many will say to Me, 'Lord! Lord! We prophesied in Your name and cast out demons in Your name and performed many miracles in Your name.' But I will reply, 'I never knew you. Get away from Me, you who break God's laws' " (Matt. 7:21-23 NLT).

From Jesus' own words we learn the importance of developing our relationship with Him. Operating in spiritual gifts is no substitute for friendship and fellowship with God and no indication of our relationship with the Lord. It doesn't matter how much we have done for Jesus. It doesn't matter if we have seen great numbers of people come to know Christ. It doesn't matter if we have healed the sick, or given accurate prophecies. God gives spiritual gifts "without repentance" and even reprobates can operate in these.

At times some people have been proven to be frauds and still have testimony after testimony of people receiving something miraculous from their "ministry." God still moves through the spiritual gifts He has given them to preach the Gospel because He loves people and wants to save them.

A person may have had an experience with the Lord, but they are false prophets if they behave in ways that are contrary to the Gospel, if they do not bring their life into submission to the word of God, and if they do not have an ongoing relationship with the

Lord. Because spiritual gifts still operate in their lives and they can still prophesy and work miracles, they falsely assure themselves, thinking that they have God's stamp of approval and that He isn't concerned about their sinful lifestyle.

John Wesley, one of the greatest revivalists of the church, commented on this possibility saying that he could lead thousands of people into heaven and be cast into hell when he was done if he did not know the Lord personally and live a godly life and keep His commandments. The Apostle Paul said it this way: "I discipline my body and bring it into subjection, that after proclaiming to others the Gospel and things pertaining to it, I myself should become unfit, not stand the test, be unapproved and rejected as a counterfeit" (1 Cor. 9:27, AMP).

Anna Mendez, an evangelist from Mexico, once told me about a vision she had seen that confirms this principle. In her vision, angels were coming from Heaven to go to a meeting. As the preacher was speaking, great works of God were taking place. People were being healed, demons were being cast out, and people were being set free by the power of the Holy Spirit. My friend asked the angels, "Who is the preacher leading the service?" An angel answered her saying, "Oh, we don't know who he is. We came because he is preaching the Word of God and proclaiming the Name of Jesus."

God always honors His Name, and His Word will not return void. He loves all people and wants everyone to come to the knowledge of the truth. However, although the minister did the works of the Lord and did great miracles, because he didn't have an intimate relationship with the Lord Jesus, the angels did not know him either.

WOLVES IN SHEEP'S CLOTHING

In the Bible, there is no such thing as a Christian who continues in rebellion against God. To be a Christian is to give up your rebellion and be a rebel no longer. There is no such thing as a partial commitment to Jesus. There are no sliding scales of percentages. There is no such thing as a Christian who gives fifty percent of his life to Jesus and keeps the other half for himself to live in any way he chooses, nor is there such a thing as a Christian who lives ninety-five percent of the time for Jesus and still lives five percent for himself.

Jesus said, "You cannot serve two masters" (Matt. 6:24). It is all or nothing! To be a real Christian is to fully surrender self and give one hundred percent of your life to the Lord. Jesus promises, "Whoever loses his life for My sake will find it" (Matt. 16:2). The cross is the place where not only Jesus died, but where we must die to ourselves, so that we can live unto God.

Paul told the Galatians, "Those who are Christ's have crucified the flesh with its affections and lusts"(Gal. 5:24). According to this scripture we can conclude that those who haven't crucified the flesh with its affections and lusts don't belong to Christ.

Jesus told us how to identify those who are false. He taught, "Beware of false prophets who come to you in sheep's clothing but inwardly are ravenous wolves. You can identify them by their fruit, that is, by the way they act" (Matt. 7:15-16 NLT).

Jesus explained that the greatest mark of His disciples will be love, "By this all will know that you are My disciples if you have love for one another" (John 13:35). Paul explains the characteristics of this love: "Love is patient and kind. Love is not jealous or boastful or proud or rude. It does not demand its own way. It is not irritable, and it keeps no record of being wronged. It does not rejoice about injustice but rejoices whenever the truth wins out. Love never gives up, never loses faith, is always hopeful, and endures through every circumstance" (1 Cor. 13:4-7).

Being full of the love of God is not something any human can produce. This kind of love is "imparted" to us by spending time in

God's Presence and being filled with His Holy Spirit. Paul tells us "the love of God is shed abroad in our heart by the Holy Spirit" (Rom. 5:5). Those who don't know Jesus cannot be filled with His love. They are just users of the powerful Name that is above every other name and fall into the category of those Jesus doesn't know. From this we learn that developing our relationship with the Lord is a crucial part of being a true Christian. The Christian life is impossible without it.

FOCUSING ON HIS PRESENCE

One of the greatest blessings of the New Covenant is the privilege of living in communion with God's Presence. Here are some concepts that will help you enter into a greater reality of this great privilege. When you pray, where do you see God? This is one of the key points to understanding and experiencing God's Presence.

Do you picture God in heaven somewhere, or do you picture Him in your heart and in everything around and within you? If you picture God as distant and far away in Heaven, you will tend to strive or speak as loud as possible to try to get God to hear you. The secret to experiencing God's Presence continually is realizing that He is present everywhere—that His Presence surrounds you and, by His Spirit, He dwells within your heart.

The concept of God being separate from you and off in Heaven somewhere is a pagan concept. When Elijah challenged the prophets of Baal to a prayer meeting on Mt. Carmel the stakes were high. The agreement: the true God would answer with fire. The prophets of Baal made their sacrifice and ranted and raved until evening. They danced around their altar and cut themselves with knives, trying to show their sacrifice and dedication, and attempted to get their god to answer from heaven.

Elijah taunted them saying, "You'll have to shout louder for surely he is a god! Or maybe he is away on a trip, or he is asleep and needs to be wakened!" When it became Elijah's turn to pray, he prepared his altar, laid the sacrificed bull on it, soaked it in water, then prayed a three-sentence prayer and God answered with a consuming fire! As a result, all of Israel fell on their faces and cried out, "The Lord He is God!" (1 Kings 18:27, 39).

Have you ever felt like the prophets of Baal when they pray? Is your view of God distant, and do you think that your loud words and actions will move Heaven? Jesus admonished, "And when you pray, do not use vain repetitions as the heathen do. For they think that they will be heard for their many words"(Matt. 6:7).

Like the prophets of Baal, people also have the false concept that the more that they sacrifice, the more they get God's attention. Jesus has already made this sacrifice and finished the work of reuniting man with God. On the cross Jesus said, "It is finished." Paul reminds us, "The person who is joined to the Lord is one spirit with Him" (1 Cor. 6:17 NLT).

GETTING RID OF THE CONCEPT OF DISTANCE

Striving in prayer can also occur when you picture demonic principalities between you and God. This concept can make you feel very distant from God and make you feel that you have to work to get these principalities out of the way so you can contact Heaven. Here is a scripture for you: "For I am persuaded that neither death nor life, nor angels nor principalities nor powers, nor things present nor things to come, nor height nor depth, nor any other created thing, shall be able to separate us from the love of God which is in Christ Jesus our Lord" (Rom. 8:38-40).

Even in the Old Covenant, God was not presented as being distant and off in heaven somewhere. The prophet Jonah thought he could take a ship and sail away from Israel and escape God's Presence. He was sorely mistaken. David wrote about the omnipresence of God: "Where can I go from Your Spirit? Or where can I flee from

Your Presence? If I ascend into heaven, You are there; if I make my bed in hell, behold, You are there. If I take the wings of the morning, and dwell in the uttermost parts of the sea, even there Your hand shall lead me, and Your right hand shall hold me" (Ps. 139:7-10). Explaining God to the unbelieving Greeks on Mars Hill, Paul continues David's theme, "He is not far from any of you, for in Him you live, move and have your being" (Acts 18:27b-28). Every fiber of the universe, every atom, every breath we take is filled with His Presence. He encompasses and fills every element of the entire universe with His Presence—the entire universe is "in Him." The Old Testament presents God as One who not only observes our actions, but also hears our words and knows our thoughts. David prayed, "Let the words of my mouth and the meditations of my heart be acceptable in Your sight, O Lord my strength and my Redeemer" (Ps. 19:14).

THE KINGDOM WITHIN

In the New Covenant, we have a greater promise than the Old. When Jesus was speaking to His disciples about leaving to go to His Father, He sensed their sadness. He promised them, "If you love Me, keep My commandments. And I will pray to the Father, and He will give you another Helper, that He may abide with you forever—the Spirit of Truth, whom the world cannot receive, because it neither sees Him nor knows Him; but you know Him, for He dwells with you and will be in you. I will not leave you orphans; I will come to you" (John 14:15-18). When Jesus commissioned His disciples after His resurrection, He gave the promise of His Presence saying, "And be sure of this: I am with you always even until the end of the age" (Matt. 28:20 NLT).

The great truth of Christianity is that not only does God surround us, He also dwells in our hearts by His Holy Spirit. Be still and know He is God. Close your eyes and as you pray, realize that God's Presence surrounds you and is within you. He is everywhere present. Just know that He is within your heart and you can find Him there.

Paul explained to the Romans, "But the righteousness of faith speaks in this way, 'Do not say in your heart, who will ascend into heaven?'(that is, to bring Christ down from above) or, 'Who will descend into the abyss?'(that is, to bring Christ up from the dead). But what does it say? 'The word is near you, in your mouth and in your heart' (that is, the word of faith which we preach)" (Rom. 10:6-8).

Asked by the Pharisees when the kingdom of God would come, Jesus replied to them by saying, "The kingdom of God does not come with signs to be observed or with visible display, nor will people say, 'Look! Here it is!' or, 'See, it is there!' For behold, the kingdom of God is within you, in your hearts and among you, surrounding you " (Luke 17:20-21 AMP).

It is this kingdom which Jesus told us to seek that carries with it His great promise, "Seek first the kingdom of God and His righteousness and everything you need will be given to you" (Matt. 6:33). When we realize God's Presence in this way and our focus becomes quiet and inward, we will stop trying to bring God down from the sky, and we will notice a change—the ability to commune with Him.

THE HEAVENS ARE OPEN

The great news about the New Covenant is that we serve the Lord under an "open heaven." When Jesus was baptized, we learn from the scriptures that the "heavens were opened" (Matt. 3:16). There is no record of them closing again. Not only that, Paul explains, "You were buried with Christ when you were baptized. And with Him you were raised to new life because you trusted in the mighty power of God, who raised Christ from the dead" (Col. 2:12 NLT).

Baptism in water is a grave where you bury the self that has died. It is the reign of "self" in my life as king and lord of all that must be buried. It is my independence from God, my right to myself that must be laid in the grave. Paul explains, "When we became Christians and were baptized to become one with Christ Jesus, we died with Him. For we died and were buried with Christ by baptism. And just as Christ was raised from the dead by the glorious power of the Father, now we also may live new lives" (Rom.6:3-4 NLT). Those who have believed and have been baptized share in His baptism, have been raised up to new life, and have the privilege of living under an open heaven.

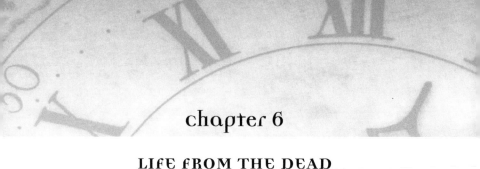

chapter 6

LIFE FROM THE DEAD

All we have to decide is what to do
with the time that is given us.

—GANDALF, THE GREY

J. R. R. TOLKIEN, *THE LORD OF THE RINGS*

As the granddaughter of the founders of Christ For The Nations, Gordon and Frieda Lindsay, Missy Lindsay grew up within a great heritage and was privileged to have what you would call "a front row seat in ministry." However, in her teen years, she was a rebellious teenager who wanted nothing to do with her family or their worldwide ministry, and she had no fear of God in her life. Boyfriends and sports were her life, but it seemed God had a different plan for her. At the age of 17, during her senior year of high school, God woke her up out of her selfish world when she was hit and literally killed by a speeding car in a hit and run accident.

MISSY LINDSAY'S STORY

On that fateful—or you could say Providential—night in early November, I had planned to visit my friends at the Christ For the Nations men's dormitory which was on a busy Dallas street. I was running by myself across the intersection when a big white Cadillac sped through the red light going between 60 to 80 miles an hour.

The car struck my leg, tore my hamstring, and threw me into the car's windshield.

The impact to my face made my forehead swell to the size of a softball. I then flew 35 feet through the air and landed headfirst on the concrete, which split open the back of my head and spilled 2 to 3 pints of blood onto the ground. It was a 'hit and run' and the Cadillac kept going, ran through another red light and left me dead—literally—without a pulse and without breath.

CFN security and paramedics confirmed I was dead at the scene and relayed the information to the hospital as they desperately tried to revive me. The students who saw the accident ran over to my lifeless body and began rebuking the spirit of death. After eight minutes, the ambulance arrived only to find that my life had miraculously returned.

When they rushed me to the hospital, I was still in an unconscious state and was not expected to live through the night. To their surprise, I regained consciousness in a day and had no broken bones. After many tests they could find nothing major wrong with me, so they sewed up my head, gave me a pair of crutches so I wouldn't put any weight on my leg, and sent me home. Being the non-Christians they were, they said, "Somebody special must be watching out for you." Those words really struck something deep in my heart, and I began to re-evaluate my life.

At the time of the accident, my parents were in Argentina. My dad had just finished preaching a sermon entitled, "God takes care of His children," when he received the news. We learned later that family intercessors, unaware of the event, had begun praying for me at the exact time of my accident. I know God miraculously intervened and protected me.

THE WAKE-UP CALL

Looking back now, I see how the Lord used this accident as a serious wake-up call from Him. God began speaking to me saying, "Missy, I didn't give you a front-row seat in ministry for nothing. I have a destiny for your life, and it's time to line up your priorities so you can take hold of that destiny. Missy, the temporal things fade away; reach for the eternal things that will never fade." At that moment, I began to realize that His grace and mercy were upon my life, and I knew that He had a great plan for me.

After I graduated from high school in the spring, I went on an outreach to Albania with Teen Mania. This experience changed my life forever. One night during my first week there, all my dirty clothes, including "all my unmentionables," were stolen. During my second week in Albania, my make-up bag was stolen, and during my last week, my big suitcase was stolen.

I came back to the States with just the "clothes on my back" – literally! I cried all the way home because I had packed my best clothes in those suitcases. It was my first outreach, and I didn't know not to take my best stuff. But again, the Lord was teaching me through adversity, saying, "Missy, temporal things are not important; it's the eternal things that matter." The message began to sink in.

I realized I needed to get a good foundation in the Word of God so I decided to attend Christ For The Nations Institute (CFNI). During my time as a student, I realized that God was calling me to give my life in the work of ministry. One of my first ministry opportunities came when I was asked to be involved with a professional acting group that performed for the three to four thousand youth who attended Youth For The Nations—a summer camp on Christ For The Nations' campus. This was definitely out of my comfort zone, but I felt I was to go and it was rewarding.

The Lord opened up another important opportunity during my time as a CFNI student. The president of Oral Roberts University (ORU), Richard Roberts, invited me to attend his university on a full scholarship. This, I believed, was to be my next step. I decided to major in Organizational Interpersonal Communication because I recognized that many of the problems people face in ministry today stem from unclear communication. I felt that if I could become a skilled communicator, I would be able to lessen my problems in the ministry or just in life itself. After graduating with my bachelors, I went on to pursue my Master of Divinity. I knew I needed to learn how to accurately study the Word of God if I intended to be skilled in further ministry work.

GETTING RID OF MY OBJECTIONS

I have to be honest. During my years at ORU, I still was fighting the idea of being a minister. First, my impressions were that ministers were poverty-stricken and penniless, often the object of mockery, jokes, and criticism. This is what I had experienced and seen growing up in the ministry. God soon removed my doubts through the understanding words of my mentors who helped me realize that this was a poverty and martyr mentality, and that I had to reject this type of limiting thinking.

Secondly, I felt as though I had no real gifts. Many well-esteemed prophets had prophesied a lot of great things over me, but I didn't believe them. I thought to myself, "They're just saying these things because they know whose child I am. The odds of ministers' children doing great things with their lives are good." I also thought that these prophets might just be saying this to benefit my parents who were also listening to the prophetic words. I said to myself, "Look at me. I can't sing. I can't preach or prophesy. What's left for me? I can't even get up in front of people to talk and make announcements. I will have an anxiety attack and fall over on stage. I'll look like a fool again just like I did when a pastor of an 8,000 member church asked me to say a few words, and all I could say was one word—'Hi.'"

For weeks I had replayed that horrific scene in my mind, and I was totally embarrassed by it. "What could I possibly do for the Lord?" I thought. "Sure, I have great God-dreams that I want to fulfill, but how can I accomplish them?" I resolved, "Well, I will just get married, and that will solve the problem. My husband can be the minister, and I can just support him. That way, I can live vicariously through him."

I admit that part of my thinking at that time was tied to a personal situation. The Student Body President of CFNI was pursuing my hand in marriage. I was desperately seeking the Lord for an answer for my future.

It was May, and I decided to take a break from the relationship and go on an outreach to Mexico for the summer. That way, I could breathe and receive some clarity for the future without day-to-day contact with this man. During the trip, the relationship fizzled out, and the Lord gave me a clear message, "Missy, I have called YOU to ministry; marriage will complement you, but not hide you from your calling."

After Mexico, I went back to ORU, completed my masters degree, and at the age of 26 came back to serve under my parents at Christ For The Nations Institute. My parents have never promoted me or favored me in anyway; they have always wanted the Lord to promote me. The Lord has helped me grow so much and in so many different areas. During these last three years, the Lord has opened many doors for me.

LIVING THE LIFE OF FAITH

The directors of our Advanced Leadership & Pastoral School recognized God's gifting and calling on my life. They mentored and groomed me in different areas to take responsibility, and then pushed me out of my comfort zone when they asked me to teach some classes. As I stepped out in faith and obedience to the Lord and my bosses, the Holy Spirit began to take over my mouth and the sessions were extra-ordinary. "My tongue," became "like the pen of a ready writer," as the Word has promised us in Psalm 45:1.

Prior to my obedience, the Lord had given me many prophetic words about God's teaching gift in my life, but I never really believed them because of fear and lies—the tools the enemy used to overwhelm me. After I stepped out in faith to teach, I began getting calls to speak in seminars and conferences not only in the United States, but in other nations as well. At the age of 29, I have traveled to over 30 nations. I now work in public relations as well as teach in our Advanced Leadership and Pastoral School, one of our five advanced schools of ministry.

My calling is to reach the young, aimless "Generation X er's and Y er's" who are without hope and purpose. This searching generation is blinded by selfish and evil desires, making them unable to know their purpose and pursue their destiny. They are wandering from one source of stimulation to the next, probing for something real to fill the void, but never finding it. Youth are desperate for real meaning and fulfillment, but they do not yet comprehend that their identity can only be realized at the cross of Jesus.

I am attempting to bridge this gap. I work at Christ For The Nations, a place full of young people! The average age is 18 to 25, and over 30,000 have graduated since the institute's inception. A total of 150 nations have been represented here at Christ For The Nations. Currently we have over 200 internationals representing over 50 nations in the student body. We have built 43 associated Bible schools globally and have helped plant over 11,600 churches in nations around the world. Here I can effect change for Christ in the youth of the nations of the world as well as in the United States. Since then, I have been privileged to invest in eternal things on outreach missions with Youth With A Mission, Teen Mania, Harvest Evangelism, and Christ For The Nations.

JESUS MY LIFE, MY ALL

I have only just begun in the calling God has upon my life, and I am doing it at a young age because I have chosen to reject that which is temporal and reach for the high calling of God—the eternal dream. "But whatever things were gain to me, those things I have counted as loss for the sake of Christ. More than that, I count all things to be loss in view of the surpassing value of knowing Christ Jesus my Lord, for whom I have suffered the loss of all things, and count them but rubbish so that I may gain Christ…Not that I have already obtained it or have already become perfect, but I press on so that I may lay hold of that for which also I was laid hold of by Christ Jesus. Brethren, I do not regard myself as having laid hold of it yet; but one thing I do: forgetting what lies behind and reaching forward to what lies ahead, I press on toward the goal for the prize of the upward call of God in Christ Jesus" (Phil. 3:7-8,13-14).

You too must reject the temporal and reach for the eternal. Believe in this great God who can do the impossible. Jesus is saying to us, "Truly I say to you, if you have faith the size of a mustard seed, you will say to this mountain, 'Move from here to there,' and it will move; and nothing will be impossible to you" (Matt. 17:20). The author of Hebrews tells us, "Now faith is the assurance of things hoped for, the conviction of things not seen" (Heb. 11:1-2).

Step out in faith and obedience into the dreams God has given you just like Abraham in the Old Testament. "By faith Abraham, when he was called, obeyed by going out to a place which he was to receive for an inheritance; and he went out, not knowing where he was going" (Heb 11:8). Things don't happen by chance; you must take your faith and put action to the dream, fixing your eyes on Jesus, the "author and perfecter of our faith" (Heb. 12:2).

"God orders your steps" according to Proverbs 20:24, but you must take the first step. We are exhorted to "hold fast the confession of our hope without wavering, for He who promised is faithful" (Heb. 10:23). In other words, if we step out in faith to fulfill the calling God has placed on our lives despite the odds against us (age, gender, race, or various hardship), God will help us reach our promised destiny. Remember, God says, "I know the plans that I have for you … plans for welfare and not for calamity to give you a future and a hope" (Jer. 29:11).

෮෨෧෨

Missy's story reminds us that God is calling us from the perplexing world of self- interest into the supernatural will of God through taking steps of faith. Why not ask God right now what step of faith He would have you take, and then take that step today?

chapter 7

DEVELOPING YOUR FRIENDSHIP
WITH THE LORD

I take my help wherever I can find it. Only one stipulation do
I make: my teacher must know God ... and Christ must be his
all in all.

If a man has only correct doctrine to offer me, I am sure to
slip out at the first intermission to seek the company of
someone who has seen for himself how lovely is the face of
Him Who is the Rose of Sharon and the Lily of the Valley.
Such a man can help me, and no one else can.

—A. W. TOZER (1897-1963)

THE KNOWLEDGE OF THE HOLY

As we pursue fellowship and friendship with Jesus, the reality of
the indwelling Christ will become a living reality in our hearts, and
we will be able to confess with Paul, "I have been crucified with
Christ. It's no longer I who live, but Christ who lives in me; and the
life that I now live in the flesh, I live by the faith of the Son of God
who loved me and gave Himself for me" (Gal. 2:20). It is only
"Christ within" who is "the Hope of realizing the Glory." (Col.1:
27 AMP).

As we spend time with Jesus daily in the "secret place" of our
heart, we have God's promise that we will "abide under the shadow

85

of the Almighty" (Ps. 91:1). Here in the secret place, we develop our friendship with God. This is the place we find our identity in Jesus. This is where all our strength comes from. This is where we receive supernatural anointing to do the impossible. This is the place of transformation.

When we worship Jesus and behold His glory, we will discover that we "are constantly being transfigured into His very own image in ever increasing splendor and from one degree of glory to another" by the power of the Holy Spirit (2 Cor. 3:18 AMP). This is the place where godly character is "imparted" to us. Godly character is not something we work at by trying to be humble, kind, and good. We actually receive "the righteousness of God" as we are changed from glory to glory supernaturally by the power of God who dwells in us as "His love is shed abroad in our hearts by the Holy Spirit."

God has called all who are in Christ Jesus to a life of "transformation" and sonship—not to a life of "reformation" and servitude. Reformation is endeavoring to live by rules and principles alone. God's commandments show us His standard of right and wrong behavior and are the foundation of our faith. The Old Covenant held the promise of life, joy, and order through keeping God's laws (Deut. 28, Ps. 19:7-11). Those who keep God's commandments will always be blessed.

However, *transformation,* in contrast, is a New Covenant promise produced by laying down the old life, and through repentance, baptism in water, and baptism in the Holy Spirit, becoming a new creation. According to New Covenant promise, those who believe receive a new nature—a new heart and a new spirit fashioned after the image of Jesus. Jesus is the Father of the New Creation.

In humble submission to the Lordship of Jesus, we worship God, gaze on His glory, and " are transformed into His image from glory to glory by the Sprit of the Lord" (2 Cor. 3:18). As we "take every thought captive to the obedience of Christ," we are "transformed by the renewing of our mind" (Rom. 12:2). Paul reminds us that we are to be "washed with the water of the word" that we might become "a glorious church without spot or wrinkle" so that we might be "holy and without blemish" (Eph. 5:25-27). We are exhorted to "lay aside all filthiness and wickedness" and "to receive with meekness the word implanted which is able to save our souls" (James 1:21).

AVOIDING DISTRACTIONS

Today, there are endless distractions that can keep us from developing our relationship with the Lord. Jesus told His disciples to be careful not to get weighed down with "the cares of this life" (Luke 21:34). If I am not careful, it is so easy to allow the business of life to distract me from God, no matter how much I want the Lord to have His way in my life. I find myself caught up with day-to-day activity—socializing, working, and entertaining myself—and before I know it, I have gotten out of the practice of being intimate with the Lord. As a result, I can easily fall into doing things without a clear revelation that comes from disciplining myself to listen to His voice in my quiet time.

If you are anything like me, at times I sometimes love to stay up late to hang out with friends, or to watch a movie, or mostly to do productive things. Doing productive things makes late nights seem even more justified. These activities are not bad or sinful things in themselves, but they can affect my relationship with the Lord.

When I end up falling asleep late, I still plan to wake up very early so I can have time to pray and seek God. However, sometimes because I am so tired, I hit the snooze button and sleep until the last possible minute. I get up just in time to take a shower, and then I have to run out the door into my busy life without receiving the power from God for that day. Although I always try to spend time with the Lord throughout the day, as well as before I go to sleep, it's not the same. However, when I spend time with Jesus in the morning, I am energized by His Presence, understand His will, and receive His empowerment for that day—my daily bread!

Jesus spoke of Himself as "the Bread coming down out of heaven" and compared Himself and the life that He gives to the "manna" the Israelites received in the wilderness (John 6:33-35). One unique thing about this manna was that it had to be gathered daily as it fell from heaven. If the Israelites tried to stock up on enough manna to last them for two or three days, it became filled with worms and was not fit to eat. We make a similar mistake when we think that we can live on yesterday's fellowship and meditation.

Procrastination can easily become a pattern as we let days go by without spending time in intimate fellowship with the Lord. Trying to make up for lost time, we are tempted to try and sandwich God in between appointments, thinking we are doing Him a favor. It's also tempting to take the time to pray and then talk the whole time and leave hurriedly without even waiting upon the Lord to speak to us.

Spending time getting to know the Lord is about communication, not a one-way conversation. A marriage or friendship would never work if only one person did all the talking and there was never any time to hear your spouse or friend's heart. Why would God want less than you would give other relationships?

Mother Teresa explains the importance of waiting quietly before the Lord:

> Jesus is always waiting for us in silence. In this silence He listens to us; it is there that He speaks to our souls, and there, we hear His voice. In this silence we find a new energy and a real unity. God's energy becomes ours, allowing us to perform things

well. There is unity of our thoughts with His thoughts, unity of our prayers with His prayers, unity of our actions with His actions, or our life with His life. Make every effort to walk in the Presence of God.[1]

Remember Jesus promised, "My sheep hear My voice, and I know them, and they follow Me" (John 10:27). Jesus also promised, "However, when He, the Spirit of Truth, has come, He will guide you into all truth; for He will not speak on His own authority, but whatever He hears He will speak; and He will tell you things to come" (John 16:13). Call on the Holy Spirit for His help. You don't have to worry that you will receive things from the devil. Jesus promised, "If you ask for a fish, He won't give us a serpent…the Father in heaven will give good things to those who ask Him" (Matt. 7:7-11).

THE IMPORTANCE OF PRAYER

Spending time in prayer is an important aspect of developing our friendship with God. When the disciples saw Jesus' relationship with the Father, they wanted to know the secret so they asked, "Lord, teach us to pray." In Matthew 6:9-15, we find the Lord's Prayer, which is the model for prayer that Jesus gave them. This model is helpful to use as a prayer guide.

As you read each part of the Lord's Prayer, stop on each thought and meditate on what it means—expand on each area in prayer and thanksgiving. For example, in the phrase, "Our Father which art in Heaven hallowed be Thy Name," you could meditate on the greatness of God the Creator of Heaven and Earth and honor His name. Begin to thank Him for all His blessings, thank Him for who He is and the fact that He lives in you, He saved you, and He called you into fellowship with Him.

One of the functions of the Holy Spirit is to help us pray. When we run out of our own words and we grasp for what to say, we are enabled to pray in even a deeper way through the gift of the Holy Spirit by praying in unknown tongues—a prayer language given to us by the Holy Spirit. Concerning prayer in the Holy Spirit, Paul teaches:

> For he who speaks in a tongue does not speak to men but to God, for no one understands him; however, in the spirit he speaks mysteries… He who speaks in a tongue edifies himself… If I pray in a tongue, my spirit prays, but my understanding is unfruitful. "What is the conclusion then? I will pray with the spirit, and I will also pray with the understanding. I will sing with the spirit, and I will also sing with the understanding.
>
> And the Holy Spirit helps us in our distress, for we don't even know what we should pray for, or how we should pray. But the Holy Spirit prays for us with groanings that cannot be expressed in words. And the Father who knows all hearts knows what the Spirit is saying, for the Spirit pleads for us believers in harmony with God's own will" (1 Cor. 14:2,4a, 14-15; Rom. 8:26-27 NLT).

To maintain our spiritual development and to intercede for the will of God, I think that it's important to follow Paul's direction to pray with your understanding and to also pray in the spirit—in tongues—everyday. Your spiritual strength will increase through your consistency in prayer.

One thing that I do when I pray in the spirit is to picture the things that God has placed on my heart. Then I just pray in tongues over my concerns while holding that image in my mind until I feel a release from the request. I believe that the Spirit of God has made intercession for each concern according to the will of God because this is what the scripture promises. Then I move on as the Spirit leads, or stop as the Spirit leads. Praying in the spirit is so important because according to the word of God, you are praying the will of God into your life and circumstances. This is one of the most powerful gifts the Lord gives us for our personal edification.

PARTAKING OF HOLY COMMUNION

A dynamic way God has provided in practicing the Presence of God is experiencing the Presence of the Living Christ though partaking of Holy Communion, or the Lord's Supper. Mystical—mysterious, God's Presence is contacted through this remembrance and gratitude.

Partaking of the bread and the wine in Holy Communion is an important ordinance that Jesus established for experiencing His abiding Presence. At the Passover supper on the night that Jesus was betrayed, Jesus broke the bread and gave it to His disciples saying, "This is My body which is given for you; do this in remembrance of Me." Likewise He also took the cup after supper, saying, "This cup is the New Covenant in My blood, which is shed for you" (Luke 22:19-20 NLT).

Jesus refers to the importance of partaking of His body and blood saying, "Unless you eat the flesh of the Son of Man and drink His blood, you have no life in you. Whoever eats My flesh and drinks My blood has eternal life, and I will raise him up at the last day. For My flesh is food indeed, and My blood is drink indeed. He who eats My flesh and drinks My blood abides in Me, and I in him. As the living Father sent Me, and I live because of the Father, so he who feeds on Me will live because of Me" (John 6:53-57).

When Jesus appeared to His disciples as a traveler on the road to Emmaus and explained the scriptures to them, they invited Him for dinner, not knowing He was the Lord. Luke tells us that when

He sat down with them at the table, they recognized Him when He broke the bread.

Partaking of the Lord's Supper was a focal point of the early church because more than anything else they longed to fellowship with the risen Christ. They understood that the Presence of Jesus was with them when they took the covenantal bread and wine. Acts records:

> Those who believed what Peter said were baptized and added to the church—about three thousand in all. They joined with the other believers and devoted themselves to the apostles' teaching and fellowship, sharing in the Lord's Supper and in prayer…And all believers met together constantly and shared everything they had…they worshiped together at the Temple each day, met in homes for the Lord's Supper, and shared their meals with great joy and generosity (Acts 2:41-42,44,46 NLT).

In the writings of the early church fathers, we find that they believed that when the bread and the wine are taken in remembrance of Jesus, the real Presence of Christ accompanies it. Both Martin Luther, leader of the Reformation, and John Wesley, leader of what historians have called the Second Reformation, emphasized the importance of the believer partaking of the Lord's Supper for maintaining and enjoying the sense of God's Presence. [2]

We are told in the book of Revelation that as a believer and follower of Jesus Christ, He has made us His priests (Rev. 1:6, 5:9-10). While it is good to take Communion with other members of the body of Christ, we can take the bread and the wine and bless it and partake of it in our personal devotions as well. At the Last Supper, Jesus told His disciples to partake of His body and His blood as often as they wished to remember Him. Sometimes when I am meditating on the Lord and spending time with Him, it takes much longer to feel His Presence than at other times. However, when I take Communion before I spend time with God, I notice a huge difference.

Before taking Communion, I ask the Lord to examine my heart and cleanse me from all sin, and then I take the bread and wine, claiming the New Covenant promises through the body and blood of Christ. I enter right into the Holy of Holies, not because of what I have done or who I am, but because of His sacrifice.

The author of Hebrews explains, "Therefore, brethren, having boldness to enter the Holiest by the blood of Jesus, by a new and living way which He consecrated for us, through the veil, that is, His flesh, and having a High Priest over the house of God, let us draw near with a true heart in full assurance of faith" (Heb. 10:19-22a). As we center on the Presence of God dwelling within us, our hearts pour out to the Lord in worship and prayer.

PRACTICAL WAYS TO STUDY THE BIBLE

As you grow spiritually, you will want to have a thorough understanding of the Bible. If you have never read the Bible from beginning to end, it is important to do so. Spiritual truth is not based on isolated verses in the Bible and must be consistent with the entire word of God. A good plan for reading the Bible through is to read three chapters in the Old Testament and one chapter in the New Testament everyday; this will take you through the entire Bible in one year.

However, it isn't enough just to read the Bible, it's important to study and meditate on God's Word. "Be diligent to present yourself approved to God, a worker who does not need to be ashamed, rightly dividing the Word of truth" (2 Tim. 2:15). In our study of the Word of God, we need to pray and ask the Lord "to give us the spirit of wisdom and revelation and knowledge of Him and that the eyes of your understanding may be enlightened" (Eph.

1:17-18a). Paul reminds us, that the natural mind cannot understand the things of God, "but God has revealed them to us by His Spirit" (1 Cor. 2:10). Before you read the Bible or any book, ask the Lord to reveal to you what He would have you know.

Another way to study your Bible is to use a Bible concordance and do subject studies. One concordance I really enjoy is the *Strong's Concordance*. Many concordances are also accessible on the web. Using this tool, look up a word that expresses a topic you would like to study, for example "purity" or "joy." In a notebook, write down the verses and the notes that God gives you on the subject. The Holy Spirit teaches comparing scripture with scripture. Paul explains, "These things we also speak, not in words which man's wisdom teaches, but which the Holy Spirit teaches comparing spiritual things with spiritual" (1 Cor. 2:13).

As you meditate on the scriptures, the word will take root in your heart. As a result, you will be shocked at how many scriptures you'll remember to refresh you in times of need. You can also get a Bible study book for a subject that's been on your heart. Jesus taught, "He who receives seed on good ground is he who hears the word and understands it, who indeed bears fruit and produces some a hundredfold, some sixty, and some thirty" (Matt. 13:22-23).

SETTING A GOAL

As you grow in your relationship with the Lord, set a realistic goal to spend time with Him when you can be alone in His Presence. If you only have 15 minutes in the morning, then great! Start a habit; it only takes 2 weeks—14 days—to form a habit. Set the time aside and stick to it. If you are having a hard time being consistent, start by spending just 15 minutes daily and begin to increase it to 30 minutes by adding a few extra minutes each day, then let it grow from there. Also know that you don't have to strive in your own abilities. Remember that Jesus called the Holy Spirit the

"Helper." He will help you in developing your relationship with the Lord. If you have 30 minutes here is a plan that may help you:

1. Pray and worship for 10 minutes
    Thank Jesus for all He has done. The Bible exhorts us to "Enter into His gates with thanksgiving and enter His courts with praise. Be thankful unto Him and bless His name" (Ps. 100:4).

    Take Communion in remembrance of our covenant in His blood. Ask the Holy Spirit to usher you into God's Presence. God is a friend of silence. Sit quietly in God's Presence. "Be still and know that He is God"(Ps. 46:10).
    Pray from the Lord's Prayer taught by Jesus in Matthew 6:9-14. Pray for God's kingdom to come and His will be done in your life. Give Him your whole day.

2. Read the Bible for 10 minutes, carefully meditating on the words.

3. Use the last 10 minutes to wait on the Lord to hear His voice.

These suggestions are not meant to be legalistic instructions, but guidelines to help you in your spiritual growth. Soon you will want to increase your fellowship time as you draw your life from His Presence. Always endeavor to be led by the Holy Spirit in everything you do. Always remember to take the time to listen to the Holy Spirit. Remember you can hear the voice of the Lord—it's part of your spiritual inheritance—don't cheat yourself out of this amazing gift! Can you imagine that the Lord, the Creator of Heaven and Earth, who is more important than the President of any nation, wants to spend time with you daily? He knows every detail about you. He wants you to know Him intimately. What a gift!

Phoebe Palmer, one of the most significant female theologians in history who taught on sanctification and played a significant role in spreading Christian holiness throughout the United States and the world in the 19th century wrote, "When God has completely captured you: your heart will be emptied of all self, you will be cleansed from all idols. You will be cleansed from all filthiness of the flesh and spirit, you will realize your dwelling in God, and He becomes the portion of your soul, your 'All in All.'" [3]

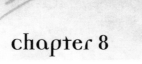

chapter 8

NO GREATER LOVE

Now abides, faith, hope, love,
these three—But the greatest is love.

—PAUL

1 CORINTHIANS 13: 13

My name is Shara Lea Pradan. I was radically saved and I am literally the first Christian in both generation lines of my family. My mother is Jewish, my father is from India, and they are both avid intellectual atheists. Having said that, my dad has always had a real compassion for the poor. Having grown up in India, he never forgot where he came from. My parents are extremely generous. My parents taught us that we should never lock our doors because if people steal from us, they need it more than we do.

My older sister is a lawyer for the U.S. Ambassador to Iraq. My family is all about social justice, changing nations, and helping third world countries; they just don't do it through Jesus. When I was four, I used to say I wanted to be the President of the United States so I could feed all the poor people. When I was seven, I remember adopting poor children who were starving to help to send money for their support.

When I was starting the eighth grade, my family moved from Massachusetts to Texas. One day at school a friend asked me, "What do you believe in?" I thought she meant politically, because

I had never seen a Bible, never been to church, and never even heard the name Jesus. I told her that I had always wanted to change the world through helping the poor, the homeless, and the underprivileged nations.

She turned to me and said, "No, I mean do you believe in God?"

That one question actually propelled my heart forward on a pilgrimage to find out if God really existed. It bothered me so much as an eighth grader that I didn't even know if I believed in God, so I went on a quest to find out if God was real or just a figment of people's imagination.

SEARCHING FOR THE TRUTH

I joined a Jewish youth group, and for nine months I spent all my free time researching every major world religion. In the middle of this search, my friend invited me to a Christian conference. At first, I only agreed to go because all my friends in a speech and acting group were going together, and I thought it would be fun to go on a trip. However in my quest for God, the night before I went to the conference I decided it might help something if I got down on my knees to pray.

I had not been taught to pray and I wasn't sure what to do, so I got down on my knees, crossed myself with the sign of the Christian cross, and said a "Hail Mary" because I had seen it on television. I said, "God, I don't believe You exist, and I feel like I'm talking to myself, but I know You are out there somewhere and I need help finding You. So please help me." Then I got up off my knees and went to bed.

The next day, I left for the conference in Texas. When I arrived at the conference I found out that it was sponsored by the Chinese churches in America who were influenced by the teaching of Watchman Nee. The auditorium was full of youth who were in the middle of a prayer meeting. They were all praying and were crying out the name "Jesus." I had never been in a Christian meeting before. I thought, "O my God, what is this?" It frightened me and I wondered if I had walked into a cult.

I had been reading in the paper about a religious cult in Waco, Texas, that had been surrounded by government tanks because they had refused to surrender their stash of weapons. As the tanks had moved in to force surrender, the buildings that the cult members were hiding in accidentally caught on fire and many people were burned alive.

I kept watching these people intently as they prayed and continually repeated the name of Jesus. Something within me wanted to just try and see if I could encounter God. I decided that I would join in, so I cried out from my heart, "Oh, Lord Jesus!" just like they were doing.

Suddenly, just by calling the name of Jesus, I was thrown back in the chair. This was a non-charismatic church so the friends that I was with were a little shocked and looked at me wondering what had happened. I felt the entire room spin, and although I didn't see Jesus, I felt the Presence of the Living God and I knew Jesus was very real. I felt the Holy Spirit infill me.

Later, I would read Paul's words in the Bible, "Whoever calls on the name of the Lord shall be saved" (Rom.10:13). That day I experienced the truth of that scripture. Later that night, a clear message of the cross was presented. I yielded my entire life to Jesus and I have never looked back since. I turned to my friend and asked, "How do you spell the name *Jesus*?" I had never seen the word Jesus written anywhere before.

Someone at the conference gave me a Bible. I stared reading it as much as I could before I went home. Before the conference was over, I had written tracts and letters about how to be saved to my parents, all my friends, all their friends, and all our relatives. I had a

Saul-Paul experience. Once I was blind, but now I could see! The Lord knew I was going to face a very difficult situation at home, so He gave me a very radical salvation experience. I knew that I knew that I had a very personal encounter with God, and no one would ever be able to talk me out of it. God was more real to me than any person. Six months later, I was baptized in water.

PERSECUTED FOR THE GOSPEL

When I arrived home, I immediately began preaching to my parents. My parents were very upset. To them believing in God was a divorce from what they believed, and a rejection of everything they had groomed me for and raised me to be. Their rejection was a very painful experience for me, but it was perfect training for what I would encounter later as a missionary. I never have faced on the field anything greater than what I have faced at home. So the Lord knows what He is doing and uses everything we go through for good.

The first six years I was a Christian, I wasn't allowed to spend time with Christian friends nor was I allowed to go to church. My family would have let me do anything but go to church. Because of their interracial marriage, they had experienced tremendous racism in Texas and had been rejected by Christians. They felt many Christians were phony and hypocrites, so I had to find God outside the church's four walls. My church was my Bible, my closet, and my Jesus.

Hearing the voice of the Lord was never a problem for me, I was born into it. It never crossed my mind that Jesus wouldn't speak to me. God met me in science class, and anywhere I went He would speak to me. I would wake up in the morning at 5 am and hide in the closet to read the Bible. My friends at school would smuggle me tapes from their church. I would sneak out in the morning in the pretext of going to early study sessions so I could go to school prayer meetings. I bought many of Watchman Nee's books and studied them. One thing Watchman Nee taught was that "to live is Christ and to die is gain." My mom found me reading this in one of his books and misunderstood and thought that this was some type of suicide manual. The division that my Christian faith brought at home continued to be painful. I have such an incredibly loving family and I never wanted to hurt them, yet it did hurt them because they continued to believe that for me to choose Jesus was to reject them.

Admittedly, some of the persecution I received was my own fault. The more my parents persecuted me, the more I preached at them. I had no opportunity to go to church, so I was not taught how I should respond to this. The more my parents resisted me, the more I rebelled against them and pressed into being more of a Christian. I judged them for their lack of Christianity. I came to realize how unfair and hypocritical my judgment was. My parents felt I was arrogant, prideful and acted as though I was better than them. I really failed at loving them unconditionally.

Since then, I have learned so much about a love that is patient and kind—a love that never fails. I have learned that the one thing that works is what Jesus did. He was love incarnate. He sat with the prostitutes and gave dignity to the poor. He took a drink of water from a Samaritan woman who was a social outcast and a moral failure. He made friends with sinners and loved them while they were yet sinners. The Lord showed me that love and humility is the way you win others, but it took a long time for me to understand that. My parents and I have reconciled since then, and I still know that one day they will come to know Jesus as their Savior and Lord.

GIVING EVERYTHING FOR LOVE

In the middle of all this, when I was 16, my dad took me to India to meet Mother Teresa. Although Mother Teresa was a Christian, my mom and dad respected her work for India's poor. My parents wanted to expose us to extreme poverty so we wouldn't become spoiled and be ungrateful. When we got to Calcutta, we had a meeting with Mother Teresa—she prayed for me and blessed me. I remembered looking at her feet that were like saucers because she had gone her whole life living among the poor without shoes and she had lost her arch.

There were many British tourists there to meet Mother Teresa as well. The whole thing upset me because I felt like this was a big tourist attraction. I felt the people who had come to see Mother Teresa were worshiping her instead of realizing that the true source of Mother Teresa's phenomenal heroic life was her relationship with Jesus Christ. I left the mission thinking nothing had happened, not realizing that I had received a major impartation through Mother Teresa's prayer.

Outside the mission I was approached by a swarm of begging kids, which is not unusual in India. I always wanted to help the poor, so I started giving my clothes, my jewelry, all my rupees (Indian money) and everything I had. All these little brown hands were stretched out all around me, and I just kept giving and giving. I felt so limited, like one drop in the ocean, and was so aware of my inability to meet their need. It was then I heard the Lord saying to me, "What is the one thing that you can give that never runs out?" I paused and thought about it for a moment. I realized I didn't know the answer. Then Jesus responded, "My love!"

I knew from that moment on I would spend the rest of my life giving out God's ceaseless, unending love, and I knew I would be a missionary. I knew I would press in to know Jesus and the power of His resurrection and the fellowship of His sufferings. What a gift this side of eternity to be able to suffer for Jesus! Every tear we shed for the cause of Christ is so precious to Him it is caught in heaven in a bottle (Ps. 56:8). This life is a gift to give to the only One who is worthy of it.

My family has been a great training ground for my evangelistic call to the mission field. The love they gave me for the poor, the burden they gave me to change the world, and my desire for social justice, the opportunity to be prayed for by Mother Teresa and to receive my call to the mission field—these were all things first planted in my life by my parents. God took my greatest fear that my family wouldn't go to heaven and gave me a great burden and a deep intercession to populate heaven and to ransack hell. God used my parent's persecution to cause me to press in to know Him more and used my time of isolation from other Christians to learn to hear His voice and be taught by the Holy Spirit.

THE PROMISED LAND

When I graduated from high school I went to Princeton University and threw myself into an "all you can eat buffet" of the Lord. I got involved in everything Christian. For me, my freedom from the control of my parents wasn't freedom to drink and party, as it is for many college students. For the first time in my life, I had the freedom to have Christian fellowship. I walked into my dorm room my freshman year not knowing if my roommate would be a Christian, and I found her reading my favorite book by Watchman Nee. I felt this was a sign from the Lord that He heard the cry of my hunger for Christian community.

I went wild at Princeton—with revival! I booked out every single meal I had to be with Christians. I joined all the Christian youth groups I could—it was like my "promised land." I didn't know at the time that Princeton was the seedbed for the Great Awakening, and it was here Jonathan Edwards, one of the leaders of the first Great Awakening, was president. What a blessing to be attending a university that was so steeped in the spiritual history of America!

While I was at Princeton, we had a 24/7 prayer meeting for 40 days. Many students on the campus were worshiping God and doing evangelistic work. We preached outside on the campus greens where we could reach the most students and publicly lifted up the name of Jesus. We had daily prayer meetings, we tag teamed and took all the classes bashing Christianity and then made a defense for professors who were trying to derail Christianity using the Bible.

My senior year I applied for and received several grants to do my senior thesis to prove that Jesus was the only God. These grants paid for all the bills I had at Princeton. After I graduated, ten of us stayed an extra year to witness and minister. Lou Engle came to Princeton for one day with Dutch Sheets and held one meeting with the campus leaders on prayer. As a result of this, there was a real shift in the atmosphere over the campus, and we had a move of God.

By now, I was very hungry to learn more about how to pray. When I had finished my year of Christian service at Princeton, the Lord sent me to Mike Bickle's "Fire in the Night" to be mentored in prayer. I did not have enough money to go to attend this prayer school, but I left Princeton believing that where God guides, He will provide. When I got to the school, I didn't have money for a hotel room so I had to sleep in my car. But soon, God miraculously met all my needs. From there the Lord sent me to be Jill Austin's personal assistant and to be mentored in the prophetic ministry.

POWER FROM ON HIGH

During all this time, I had been going to the best conferences in America, but I began to see a contradiction between the Christianity that I was experiencing, and the Christianity of the book of

Acts. I wanted to see miracles and the mighty power of God. I wanted to experience the power of the early church.

The Lord gave me what I had been seeking—I was invited to go to a crusade in Malawi, Africa, held by Todd Bentley. I was so thankful and excited about this opportunity. I was not sure what would await me there, but I couldn't wait to see. The first night I attended the crusade, I saw vast throng of 100,000 people blanketing the soccer field waiting to hear the Good News. The people were very, very poor. Malawi is among the three poorest nations in the world. It was here I saw my first miracle.

As I watched the crowds at the crusade, suddenly I literally saw Jesus walk through the crowd. Wherever He walked, the crowd instantly parted to the right and left, sort of like the parting of the Red Sea. The people were instantly healed with one touch of the Master's garment, like the woman with the issue of blood in the book of Luke. I stood in awe of Him. Then, I saw Heidi Baker kiss a deaf baby, and the baby's ears popped opened. These were the first actual miracles I had ever seen.

During this outreach, we were in Muslim schools doing games for the kids. I felt the Lord say, "There is one Muslim girl here that you need to share the Gospel with. She wants to accept Me, but if she does, because she is a Muslim, her life will be on the line and she could be killed."

I didn't know which girl it was, but I looked around and felt drawn to a girl, so I walked over to her and started asking her questions. As I was talking to her, I realized that she was the one the Lord was talking about. I took her on the bus and presented the Gospel to her for over an hour. She was so afraid because she knew she could loose her life if she accepted Jesus. However, just before she had to go, she prayed and asked Jesus to forgive her sin and to come into her heart. As she got off the bus, I shouted out for her to come to the crusade that night.

I was very worried about her, and I was afraid she would be killed when people found out about her conversion. That night I knew there would be 100,000 people at the crusade; if she did come, I felt it would be impossible to ever find her in such a crowd. But another miracle—I looked out the window as the bus pulled up that night, and there, standing right in front of me, was the girl with her mother, her sister, and her grandmother.

I jumped out and ran up to greet them. As I talked to them, I found out that the girl's mother and sister had full-blown aids. Her mother was in the last stages and had lost her eyesight. I really wanted to see these people healed so they would know for sure that Jesus was the Savior of the world. I tried every prayer and every healing model I could think of, but nothing worked and they were not healed. I prayed for them for over an hour.

Finally, I had to go help with the crusade. I was so upset as I went on the stage with the rest of the team. I said, "Lord Jesus, they had the courage to come here. You have to show them you are the God who saves." I was silently worshiping Jesus with tears streaming down my face. All I could hear was one word "prostitute." I argued with God about how I couldn't ask the woman if she was a prostitute and insult her like that. But the impression would not go away.

Finally, I stepped off the stage and walked over to my new friends. As I asked the lady if she was a prostitute, tears filled her eyes. She said her Muslim husband sold her and her daughters into prostitution before he died and that is why she had aids. She prayed with me and asked God for forgiveness, and at that moment she was totally healed of blindness and aids. This was the very first miracle that I had seen as a result of my prayer and my obedience to the Lord.

I wondered, "Lord, what is it in the heart of the poor that causes you to rend the heavens and come down?" I realized this was because they are not proud and were fully aware of their need for God. Jesus said, "Blessed are the poor in spirit, for theirs is the kingdom of heaven" (Matt. 5:3). Then the Lord said to me, "Within a year, you are going to give up everything you have and move to Mozambique, in southeast Africa, and become Heidi Baker's personal assistant." I really didn't know who Heidi Baker was—I had only seen her three times. Before the year was up, that word came to pass, and I got on a plane and moved to a country where I had never been before.

FORSAKING ALL I TAKE HIM

When I surrendered to God's call to go to Mozambique and assist Heidi, I thought I would probably never get married and would be a martyr. To go to Mozambique required a greater level of consecration for me. This required that I yield myself in total surrender to Jesus by emptying out everything of myself, so God could fill me. I wanted to go to a deeper place of utter dependency on the Lord. In the West there are a lot of churches, a rich Christian community, every kind of book and tape, but I wanted to take my Bible and meet my God and become poor in spirit so I could receive more of Him.

When I arrived, I didn't know anyone in Mozambique and I didn't know how to speak the language. We barely had electricity and running water. Heidi was my only friend and she was gone a lot. This wasn't just a place of physical hardship—this was a place of solitude with the Lord. Phone calls were practically impossible because they were so expensive. The loneliness of the mission field drove me to His heart. Everyday I would walk on the beach and cry because I was so lonely, but the Lord would romance me. I started walking out all the years of revelation I had received about having an intimate relationship with the Lord.

I felt the reality of Paul's words—"In everything we do we show that we are true ministers of God…as unknown, and *yet* well known; as dying, and behold we live; as chastened, and *yet* not killed; as sorrowful, yet always rejoicing; as poor, yet making many rich; as having nothing, and *yet* possessing all things" (2 Cor.6:9-10). God honored me, because in coming to Mozambique I had gained Christ.

Here in Mozambique the people are very poor. We have to have miracles because no one can afford medicine. The Bakers are living totally by faith and are feeding 50,000 people every single day and caring for thousands of children. Provision follows vision. I have seen money and food show up and multiply.

One time Heidi was going through the hardest trial of her life. I had absolutely no money and the Lord told me to go to the most expensive hotel and buy Heidi and her family Christmas presents. I did not know how I would pay for this, but I kept feeling this was what God wanted me to do. Our God is extravagant. I knew that the same God who can feed the starving could take care of presents for the Bakers.

When I got to the gift shop, I asked the Lord what He would like for me to give to the Bakers. As He told me each gift to choose, I loaded the counter with presents. Still not knowing how I would pay for them, I reached into my purse, opened my empty wallet, and there was a $100 bill. I owed $99. God gave me over and above what I needed.

In Mozambique, besides working for Heidi, I work with the orphans—they are orphans no longer. I have 20 boys I am responsible for. Every weekend when I am home, I have a chicken meal for my kids, which they love. I had one boy with me who we had found in the bush. He was starving, and his belly was bloated. That child totally recovered and never refused a meal. This time he sat in my lap and wouldn't eat; instead he just kept kissing my cheeks.

More than anything else, these children are hungry for love. I have learned that the admonition in James is true, "Pure and genuine religion in the sight of God the Father means this—caring for orphans and widows in their distress and refusing to let the world corrupt you" (James 1:27 NLT).

These children are so joyful, but they don't have anything. If you ask any of them if they are an orphan, they will say, "No, I have a Father in heaven Who supplies all my needs." One day, one of our children centers got a hole blown in the roof by ammunition that had gone off in the town because of the heat. The children were not hurt and for hours the kids sat there, looking at the gaping hole in the roof, worshiping God and thanking Him for life, the sunshine, beans and rice, for Himself. I had just returned from spending two months traveling with Heidi. I saw the best worship available in the West, but the worship with those children was more heavenly than anything that $20,000 worth of sound equipment and lights in the West could produce.

GIVING YOUR ALL FOR LOVE

What has God done in my heart since I've been in Mozambique? He has reduced me to love. I must decrease so He may increase. I thought I had so much when I came here. But He let that "grain of wheat," which was my life, "fall to the ground and die" so there might be a harvest of Him. Witchcraft is strong here, and the only thing that works is the anointing of the Holy Spirit. I am learning to live a life that is "not by might, not by power, but by the Holy Spirit"—all I want is Him and His presence.

I feel God has put me in the perfect pressure cooker, stripped me of man-made ministry, an agenda, selfish ambition, and everything but the purity of devotion. I feel like I have almost been saved again because I have been reduced to love. Jesus is teaching me to live the Sermon on the Mount, to see Him each and every day in the eyes of others. I want to make Him my everything. I want to be as close to Jesus as possible. I have no desire for any earthly glory. He is my portion and my exceeding great reward. I am happy in this season of my life.

My burden is still for the youth. I believe God wants to raise up a youth army to save the world. I want to get my masters degree at Yale and to reach India with film. I have dreams for China, for Israel, and for revival and awakening on the campuses in the United States. I preach on campuses every chance I get—I know that the future world leaders are there. I want to see them saved and go and change the world for Jesus.

I know the visions that God has given me will be fulfilled in His time. I know there is no hope for any of these dreams aside from the power of the Holy Spirit. And I know that God is looking for believers so full of the Presence of God that people are affected just by their presence as demonstrated in the life of Charles Finney during the Second Great Awakening. Because of the Presence of God he carried within, people would often fall down on their knees and repent when he would walk into a factory or when his train passed through town.

I think if I had stayed in the States I would have had a tendency to try to build my name and ministry. God in His mercy and kindness saved me from myself and taught me what the real Gospel is all about—love. The true mark of greatness in heaven is intention and how we treat others when no one else is watching, how we treat others when we can get nothing from it. I have had my life threatened, almost been jailed, lived totally on nothing, but I have met Jesus and there is nothing in the world I want but Him. I feel I don't want to leave Heidi until I can walk in the same anointing for miracles filled with the presence of God's love.

I believe if those in my generation will lay down their lives to serve others, it is the greatest path to leadership. We should not seek to be served, but to serve. Jesus taught, "You know that the rulers in this world lord it over their people, and officials flaunt their authority over those under them. But among you it will be different. Whoever wants to be a leader among you must be your servant, and whoever wants to be first among you must be the slave of everyone else (Mark 10:42-44 NLT). We have forgotten the purpose of Christianity is to lay down our lives for love, for "God is Love." Jesus taught, "Greater love has no man than this than he lay down his life for his friends." So release your dreams to God and throw yourself into serving—lay down your life in love for someone else.

God will give you as much of Him as you want, but He can't give it to you as long as there is anything of self that is unsurrendered. Surrender completely. I found what Heidi says is true— "God wants to love you to death, to kiss you to life." Nothing will satisfy but Him.

Save yourself decades in chasing after ministries and trying to become someone big in the eyes of the world or other Christians. Seek the face of the Lord until you are so pregnant with His Presence and so changed into His image that the world is changed— because when they see you, they see Him. Give yourself unreservedly to the uncreated God, anything less is a waste of time. The Bible is continuing in your life—there are stories of the acts of God yet to be told and yet to be written. Nothing will be impossible. Get rid of selfish ambition. All fruitfulness flows from intimacy— give yourself to the pursuit of Him.

ᏚᎧ᙮᎒ᎯᏅᏔ

Shara's testimony reminds me of these words from Mother Teresa:

When I was homeless, you opened your doors.
When I was naked, you gave me your coat.

When I was weary, you helped me find rest.
When I was anxious, you calmed all my fears.

When I was little, you taught me to read.
When I was lonely, you gave me your love.

In a strange country, you made me at home.
Seeking employment, you found me a job.

When I was Black, or Chinese, or white, and
Mocked and insulted, you carried my cross.

When I was aged, you bothered to smile,
When I was restless, you listened and cared.

When I was laughed at, you stood by my side,
When I was happy, you shared in my joy. [1]

"As you have done it unto the least of these, you have done it unto
Me."

—Jesus
Matthew 25:40

chapter 9

WHAT IF?

Twenty years from now, you will be more disappointed by the things that you didn't do, than by the ones you did do. So throw off the bowlines. Sail away from the safe harbor. Catch the trade winds in your sails. Explore. Dream. Discover.

—MARK TWAIN

I have learned to base my life on faith in Jesus! Ever since I can remember, and actually before I was born, my family has lived by faith for financial support, for the instructions on what He has shown us to do, and for everything else in-between.

Walking and living by faith in God and being led by His Spirit is one of the most important aspects of our Christian life. This is what sets you apart from living just an ordinary life and leads you into supernatural living. Your faith in God's promises and power will enable you to do the things you could never do in your own strength.

Your faith will grow the more you move and operate in it. If you stop using your faith in a positive manner for the advancement of the kingdom of God, unbelief will set in and cause your faith in God and His promises to shrink like an unused muscle, and consequently it become harder and harder to use.

LIVING BY FAITH, WHAT DOES IT MEAN?

What does it mean to live your life by faith? The Scriptures tell us, "Now faith is the substance of things hoped for and the evidence of things not seen" (Heb. 11:1). To live your life by faith is to live not by what you see, but by the word you know the Lord has spoken to your heart and by His promises recorded in the Bible. Paul reminds us, "For we were saved in this hope, but hope that is seen is not hope; for why does one still hope for what he sees? But if we hope for what we do not see, we eagerly wait for it with perseverance" (Rom. 8:24-25).

If you are a person who has to see it to believe it, then you won't be able to live a life of total trust in God's faithfulness without this mindset being changed. "By faith," we are told, "Abraham obeyed when he was called to go out to the place that he would receive as an inheritance. And he went out, not knowing where he was going. For he looked for the city which has foundations, whose builder and maker is God" (Heb. 11:8, 10).

I am not suggesting that you should go out "not knowing" where you are going just because Abraham did, but notice that Abraham went out when he was called. He obeyed God's call and left Ur. God had not given him the rest of the instructions, and Abraham didn't really know what the full plan was. Abraham had to obey God step by step and wait on Him for direction.

God doesn't give you a detailed plan that you can always see, or a "cradle to the grave" security plan. He gives you His word and His promise, and you must put your trust in Him. If He gave you a detailed plan to follow, why would you need to develop your friendship with God and spend time in His Presence listening to His voice? You could just follow the map or the set of rules and wouldn't need God at all.

BEHOLDING THE INVISIBLE

Let's look at Abraham's example and see what he hoped for and set his faith on. Abraham wasn't depending on what he could do in his own strength or in his own self-effort. The Bible tells us that Abraham "was looking for a city which has foundations, whose architect and builder is God" (Heb. 11:12 NAS). Abraham was looking for what God could do. He was looking for the invisible to invade the visible, the supernatural to invade the natural. This is what a life of faith is all about.

Everything God is doing is to bring man back in union with Himself. God has designed a life of following Jesus to be an adventure full of excitement, trust, hope, faith, and sometimes danger as He unfolds the plan and gives the provision along the way. The journey is not for those who are faint-hearted.

We must remember that God, who is love Himself, does not hesitate to lead us in a path that can leave us like Moses as he stood with the Red Sea in front of him, with Pharaoh's army chasing him from behind, and the Spirit of God commanding him to move forward. There was no way out but to look to God for deliverance. The Psalmist declared, "Your road led through the sea, your pathway through the mighty waters—a pathway no one knew was there" (Ps 77:19). God's provision was in the sea where He had made a way of escape, but it took God's miracle power to reveal it.

One time, my parents were planning a conference in India. My dad had to raise a lot of money for the conference. He knew God had told him to go there and train youth for ministry, but the night before all the money was due in for the conference, he was $150,000 short. He prayed and asked God, "What should I do?" God told him to send a fax to a young pastor in Taiwan who became a Christian though our ministry while he was a student in the United States, and just ask him to join with us in prayer for the $150,000 that was needed by the next day.

The very next day they received a return fax from this young man. He stated that his Buddhist relatives were so thrilled with the life changing experience that the young man had while when he was a student in the U.S., they wanted to give the entire $150,000 for Dad to reach the Hindus for Jesus! The conference was fully paid for. As a result, over 12,000 Christian youth in India who came to the conference from many different cities and from many denominations had their lives completely changed. Over 8,000 students were baptized in the Holy Spirit, and 4,000 were called by God to go into full-time ministry.

Using your faith to trust in God is the way you experience the Presence of God; it's how you receive God's promises. When a difficult situation arises, the goal is not to see how you can get though it in your own strength, but to realize that the difficulty presents you with an opportunity to see God's power and see Him move supernaturally in your life.

FAITH FOR THE MIRACULOUS

Some of my fondest memories of faith were my experiences on mission trips to Russia. Since I was five-years-old, my family has traveled back and forth many times a year to Russia to train and equip students who were just coming to know Jesus as their personal Lord and Savior. The Iron Curtain had fallen and a great awakening had broken out in this Communist land. Through a strategic plan the Lord gave to my dad, we were able to see tens of thousands of students saved there and hundreds of churches started.

When I was about nine-years-old, I was in Russia with my parents at a youth training conference. One afternoon, I was playing on the playground when I saw a mother pushing her three-year-old son in a wheelchair beside me. So I ran over to her and said, "Hey! Ma'am! Come with me and I will have my dad and all these preachers that have come with us from all over the world for a conference pray for your son and he will be healed!" Fortunately this Russian lady spoke English. She informed me that her husband was a professor at the University of Moscow and that they, or at least he was an atheist. "Well," I thought to myself, "that's ok—he won't be for long."

The lady agreed to come with me anyway. I took her into the hotel and looked everywhere, but I couldn't find one person who had come with us from the United States. I don't know why I was by myself because one of the Russian students was supposed to have been with me on the playground, but I was always very independent, even as a small child.

Finally, I got so frustrated I said, "Well, I guess I will just have to pray for him myself!" Because of my faith in God's promises, I pulled that little boy out of the wheelchair and told him to walk in the name of Jesus. I just knew it was the way Jesus would have done it. At first, I had to teach him how to put one step in front of the other because he was a paraplegic and had never walked before, but a few steps later he was walking!

I told his mom to bring her son back to the conference later on that night, and we would show the students at the conference that her son got healed to help build their faith and to show them what God can do. So she listened to me, even though I was a little girl of nine, and brought her son back to the meeting that evening. That night, I was standing behind the stage with my mother when the lady and her little boy showed up. My mother sent me out on the stage to give the testimony. That little boy ran across the platform to me, and when he did his mother dropped to her knees on stage in front of all the students and cried out to accept Jesus into her heart!

God wants to heal people and do things for them, and He wants His children to be the carriers of His Presence. He wants to use us to do it—but we have to step out in faith and believe! We can't be afraid and question, "What if nothing happens?" or think "I don't want to disappoint this person or myself." We should not consider the opinions of men. It's up to God what happens, not us. We are not the ones performing the miracle; God is, so that takes all the stress off us. We don't have to perform anything! We must be careful not to stand in the way of God; we are to be the facilitators of what God wants to do!

EXPECTING MIRACLES

We are to use our faith as a channel to release the power of God into the earth. God not only wants to see our faith, but it is our faith that sets His creative power into motion. Remember Jesus himself could only do a few miracles in Nazareth because of their unbelief. God wants to know that we believe that "He is the rewarder of those who diligently seek Him" (Heb.11:6), and that He will do what He says He will do.

Every time we went to Russia, my siblings and I were always right there with my parents praying for the sick. I remember person after person being healed—I just expected it to happen. If a person who was deaf came up to me to pray for them, I would just snap my fingers in their ears until they could hear, and then have the attitude of "Next!" I knew that my Jesus had the power to heal anything. Blind person after blind person and people with many other problems were healed instantaneously as God "confirmed His word with signs following."

I remember one young man around 19-years-old who had come to our conference. Someone had given him a Benny Hinn tape of miracles. The young man watched it many times and then went out to preach the Gospel and work miracles in the mighty name of Jesus. He just thought that was the way it was done and that's what Jesus told all Christians to do. In six months, he had started a church filled with thousands of people.

My parents always taught me that I had the same Holy Spirit as they did living in me, so any word that I received from the Lord for people, or anything at all I felt led to do, I should do. This thought has really made me who I am, and I know I have the same power and authority that Jesus promised to all those who believe (Mark 16:18). I know that I can hear God for myself, I know what He is saying, and I do it.

CALLED TO PREACH THE GOSPEL

When I was 11-years-old, Jesus had me do something different in Russia than I had ever done before. One morning, I was at our conference and I felt Jesus tug on my heart and say, "Evangeline, I want you to have your own seminar, and I want you to preach on faith." The conference had already started; we had invited speakers from all around the world to preach at this conference.

I went to my dad and said, "Dad, God told me I am to preach on faith and have my own seminar." My dad looked at me and asked, "Evangeline, do you have any notes on the subject?" I told him I had lots of notes. Actually, I had a lot of notes and points on faith that I had studied on the airplane on the way over. Most of them I had written down from hearing my dad preach on faith so many times.

"Well," he asked, "are they in Russian?" "No," I answered, "but I will have them in Russian by the end of the service!" None of the other speakers had to have their notes in Russian so I think he was trying to think of something that would be difficult for me to do so he wouldn't have to say no because of my age. However, one thing I had was a lot of faith. Because I had heard the Lord tell me to do this, the requirement to have my notes in Russian didn't faze me in the least.

I ran to the office to have the secretary translate my notes for me into Russian. At the end of the meeting as my dad was going to announce the speakers for the workshops, I ran up to my dad and held up my notes and said, "I have them!" My dad was surprised. He went over to my mom and asked her what she thought about me doing a workshop. She told him that she felt I shouldn't do it because no one would want to come hear an eleven year old and she thought that I would be discouraged. Then my dad asked the Lord what to do, and the Lord told him that if the students see a little eleven year old girl preach and move in the Holy Spirit then they would have no doubt in their minds that they could do it too! My dad turned to me and said, "Evangeline, come up here and announce your seminar!"

I was so excited. I went out on the stage with all the speakers and introduced my seminar, "I am going to give you seven keys to grow your faith and change your nation and world!" When it was time for my workshop, I remember sitting in the smallest room of all. They had given me this room because they didn't think I would have many people. Five people had gotten there early. I was excited that five people had come.

Well, soon the room was so full of people that people were sitting in widow sills, were looking in from outside, and were standing in every square inch of space. The room was filled to over-flowing! This was one of our smaller conferences with about 700 in attendance. There were over 350 people inside and outside this tiny room—over half the conference had come to my seminar.

I still remember that hour and a half seminar like it was yesterday. The Holy Spirit really showed up. At the end of the meeting, I lined up all the university students in the hallway outside. I had been to all the Rodney Howard-Browne meetings and seen it done. So I just prayed for each one of them. The Spirit of the Lord fell on them; they fell out under the power of God and received the joy of the Lord as they laughed away all the sorrow of Communism.

While I was praying for the students, two young Russian girls from the ballet school that was in the same building as our conference walked by and saw people being filled with the joy of the Lord. One of the girls was about my age and her friend was 12. The ushers had been letting the girls come to our meetings. They started following me around. Finally they asked me if I would pray for them. I laid hands on them and they fell out in the power of the Holy Spirit. The seminar turned into a revival meeting that lasted for hours.

PERSECUTED FOR THE GOSPEL

The next morning, my dad came up to me and said, "Come on Evangeline, we have to go meet with the Governor's Assistant for Religious Affairs. You got us in trouble yesterday." Later we learned from the Russian pastors that this same religious official had worked for the Soviet government in the past and had relentlessly persecuted the Christians during the Communist era.

I still remember walking into that room where this huge bald-headed Russian official was sitting. A lady sat next to him and typed every word spoken. A number of the Russian pastors were sitting around the table also. We sat down and the Governor's Assistant started ranting and raving at my dad about the two girls that I had prayed for the night before.

The official told us that the girls were the daughters of two of the leaders of the Communist party in the city, and their parents were enraged. The girls had come home from our meeting talking about their experience, and their parents said they had been up all night speaking in a language that they couldn't understand and that the girls were delusional.

The Governor's Assistant of Religious Affairs started yelling at my dad saying, "Who is this person that has done this terrible thing to these girls and ruined all the peace of Russia?" He threatened, "I am going to put this on every news channel and newspaper in Russia and I will have these churches shut down!"

Everyone pointed at me. My dad pointed at me too and said, "This young girl is the one who prayed for the girls." I was only eleven and small for my age. The religious official started turning all shades of red. I am sure he felt ridiculous, but he still kept shouting threats saying he was going to close down the churches.

Suddenly, the power of the Holy Spirit fell on my dad. My dad retorted, "If you try to shut down the churches, I am going to call every news channel in America and have it broadcast all over the United States and Europe that Russia is claiming to have religious freedom, but refuses to let a little girl pray for Russian children." At this time in history, this was wisdom from the Lord because Russia was trying to establish a friendship with the United States and was trying to show they were a free society. It was important to them to make a good impression on the West, and they were concerned about the way they were viewed by the rest of the Western world.

The Russian official sat quietly for a few moments and then said, "Well after thinking this over, I think I will change my mind. I've decided not to make a report or do anything to the churches after all."

After we walked out of that situation my dad looked at me and said, "That's pretty good, Evangeline. That's the first time you've ever preached, and you're already getting persecuted!"

ASK AND YOU WILL RECEIVE

If there is something you are believing for in your life, be specific, write it down, and ask the Lord for it. Jesus told His disciples, "Up until now you have asked Me for nothing. Ask so that your joy may be full" (John 16:24). Jesus wants us to have His joy, and Jesus said joy comes from receiving what we have asked for.

Later, John qualifies those who will receive, "And whatever we ask we receive from Him, because we keep His commandments and do those things that are pleasing in His sight" (1 John 3:22). To receive what you ask for from God, first be sure that you are keeping His commandments and doing the things that please Him. Then ask in prayer and claim God's promises.

Anytime you need more ability to have faith and trust in God, ask. Having asked, then step out in faith and believe that you have received. Remember you have to exercise your "muscle" of faith, and then it will grow! How do you exercise your faith? By looking at the circumstances that seem impossible and telling that mountain to move. Speak like you want to see it done! Your faith-filled words will set spiritual things into motion and enable the circumstances to change.

Many people simply wait around and believe that some day if they get near a great man or woman of faith, that person's faith will either rub off on them, or will be imparted to them when a person of faith prays for them. Of course, someone can pray for you to receive the gift of faith. This will help activate and increase the measure of faith that God has already given you, but you still have to use the gift of faith in order for it to increase and become great faith! You have to build your faith by stepping out in obedience to God time and time again. Dr. Martin Luther King gives us the key to how he accomplished the purposes of God for his life—"Take the first step in faith. You don't have to see the whole staircase. Just take the first step."

A Demonstration of the Power of God

When I was 14, I was preaching in Indonesia at my parent's conference. There I saw a mighty demonstration of the power of

God. Everything was going as planned when a young woman in my seminar on faith fell on the ground convulsing. Everyone started crowding around her and saying that she had a lung problem and was dying. I was a little nervous at first. I didn't want someone to die in my meeting. I ran off the stage over to where the young woman was lying on the floor. Everyone in the room was crowded closely around her.

I knelt down beside this petite girl and started commanding the sickness to go. She looked away from me. As she quickly turned her head back to look at me, the look in her eyes changed to a demonic presence. She reached up and started trying to choke me. Several people grabbed her arms and hands and held her down. At first, I moved back. Then suddenly, the Spirit of God rose up inside of me and I began to cast out that demonic presence. As the demon left her, she threw up three drops of dark blood in three evenly placed spots. I wondered what that meant.

After the seminar was over, the young woman came up to me and told me that she had been dedicated to Satan as a baby by her grandfather, who was a witchdoctor. She explained that he had dedicated her with three drops of animal blood—a bat, a cat, and a fox. This is the blood that she threw up when the demonic presence left her. She told me that she had a lung problem ever since that evil dedication. She had tried to get free before, but was not able to. The Lord had answered her prayer. She had been set free and healed by the power of the Holy Spirit!

THE BABE FACTOR

When Jesus sent out the seventy to preach, he anointed them to heal the sick and to say, "The kingdom of God has come near to you." They returned rejoicing saying, "Lord, even the demons are subject to us in your name." Jesus rejoiced in the Spirit and said, "I thank You, Father, Lord of Heaven and Earth, that You have hidden these things from the wise and prudent and revealed them to *babes*"

(Luke 10:1-21). Jesus rejoiced in the fact that the young people who followed Him were able to do these miracles. In fact Jesus proclaimed, "These signs shall follow those *who believe*. In my Name they shall cast out demons, speak with new tongues...and lay hands on the sick and they shall recover" (Mark 16: 17-18). It is not necessary to be a theologian, a mature preacher, or to be a Christian who has gone through trials for many years. The only qualification Jesus gave to operate in miracles is to be a believer.

Many people are hindered from taking that first step of faith that will bring God's power into action because they are worried about making a mistake. God would rather have you take a step of faith and be wrong than to be bound up by unbelief and fear and not step out at all. It is easier for God to align us with His plan when we are using our faith than when we are not using our faith at all.

Faith is like oxygen, we don't see it, but we have confidence that it is there. I don't have a doubt in my mind that when I take a breath there will be oxygen to fill my lungs. I don't need someone else to tell me that I am using oxygen, nor to believe for that oxygen. I just know it is there—I feel the evidence of it—I am living and breathing. Faith is as easy as just believing and just knowing! God is a covenant keeping God and He is faithful! Faith is not about striving and straining, trying to believe God's promises are true. It is about just accepting the truth because God is Truth Himself. He has promised it, and I just accept it.

It's the same with boldness. We always think that one day someone will pray for us, and then suddenly we will turn into a person with super strength. No, we have to exercise our faith to grow in boldness. We must get out of our comfort zone and just go ahead and do what God asks us to do, regardless of the consequences, regardless if others may think that we are foolish. Each time we see God act on our behalf, our boldness increases. Each experience makes it easier as our boldness grows, and each step of faith builds on another to help us have greater boldness for the bigger circumstances!

chapter 10

WHERE DREAMS BECOME REALITY

> Religion that God our father accepts as pure and faultless is
> this: to look after orphans and widows in their distress and to
> keep oneself unspotted from the world.
>
> —JAMES 1: 27

The following is the story of Andy Smith, a modern-day dreamer from the UK, who stepped out in faith to see what one of the national newspapers reported as "one of the darkest, most dangerous places in the country" transformed by the Living Christ.

ANDY'S STORY

When I was 21, I moved onto the Alton Estate, Roe Hampton in Southwest London, to share a flat (apartment) with some friends. This was one of the poorest public housing projects (called an "estate" in the UK) that had some of the highest levels of child deprivation, teenage pregnancies, and crime in our nation. It is one of the largest council housing estates in Europe where thousands and thousands of people live closely together in high-rise blocks of flats with very little opportunity or provision.

Pensioners, who live alone in isolation and fear of crime, occupy twenty-five percent of the homes. These elderly and frail people stay inside their flats, just staring at the same four walls day after day, year after year, with very little contact with the outside world. Most children in the estates grow up in workless households with only one parent at home.

My friends and I chose this area simply because it was the cheapest place to rent. At the time, I was on a very low income and did a few odd jobs—window cleaning and a bit of gardening. Together with my flat mates, I started a cell group (prayer group) in my flat. The aim was to pray and see the kingdom of God come to our friends and our area. After a couple of years, God began to challenge me and put a dream in my heart to see this estate transformed by the Gospel.

God challenged our small group asking, "How can you just continue to pray, worship, learn from the Bible, and expect to see the kingdom of God come to your area without doing anything about the problems on the estate yourselves?"

God was looking for someone to be an expression of His love; He was asking, "Where are My hands and feet on the Alton Estate? Some of the elderly are on the verge of suicide, and most are so isolated and fearful—who will befriend them?" By the age of nine, children here know how to steal mopeds and cars, they are kicked out of school and are in trouble with the police. God was asking us, "Who will be a role model for these children?"

THE DREAM BEGINS

In January 2000, at the age of 24, with the help and prayers of my Mum and of the guys in our cell group, along with the support of the other local churches, we set up a registered charity called Regenerate.com. The local council miraculously gave us some funding to open a lunch club for the elderly on the estate.

On the day of the launch party, we had about ninety elderly people gathered together for the start of what was to change many of their lives, giving them back community and friendships. The lunch club became the base for our work in demonstrating God's love to the people of Roehampton. Jesus taught, "Let your light shine, that people will see your good deeds and give praise to your Father in heaven" (Matt. 5:16). We were about to do just that.

One day an elderly lady, who carried a gun in her handbag for protection, had come into the lunch club. Something had upset her and she was so angry with God that she broke a cross that was inside her flat. She felt guilty and was nervous about coming into the lunch club. While she was eating, the Spirit of God fell upon her, and she saw the words "You're forgiven" literally appear in front of her. She went on to join a church and got baptized.

Another old lady who was completely un-churched said to me one day with tears in her eyes, "Through coming to the lunches, Jesus has come into my heart!" As far as I'm aware, we'd never spoken to her about Jesus. She also went on to join a church.

One day we came across a very old and frail lady who hadn't been out of her house for over two years. She had no family in this country, no friends, and felt so alone from having nothing to do except stare at the same four walls every day. Her last year of life was dramatically different. We took her to lunch four times a week, and we took her on a couple of afternoon trips a week. One day, not long before she died, she grabbed my hand very tightly and was crying as she tried to speak. She just kept repeating, "Andy, I'm so happy, I'm so happy!"

GOD'S PROVISION

After setting up the lunch club, I was dreaming of how we could reach more isolated, elderly people. One day I got a phone call from someone from the public health service saying that they liked what we were doing and asking if there was anything we wanted. I told them that we'd like to have a minibus to pick people up and money to employ workers to help bring people to lunch and take them out to places of interest. Not long after that conversation, the public health service gave us the money to do all of this.

We also wanted to reach young people and give them opportunities, activities, and role models that would change the course of their lives. We employed a mate (friend) of mine three days a week to help set up clubs and work in a school that was failing and struggling to stay open. We had no money to pay him, but at the end of every month the money came in somehow.

One girl who came to our clubs had struggled at home and at school. She found herself homeless by the age of thirteen, slept on different people's couches, and rarely went to school. Because this girl had severe behavioural problems, she was a very difficult person to work with. We took her on two activity holidays, and on both occasions she was sent home because her behaviour was so unacceptable.

One day we returned home from an outing, and we were very surprised to find her pushing elderly people around in their wheelchairs and helping out in our lunch club. We talked and decided to give her a mentor so she could become a volunteer and work with our elderly people. She did so well, we ended up employing her, and for two and a half years she has been one of our members of staff at Regenerate.com[1] helping to transform the lives of others. A friend of hers, who was also made homeless by the age of fifteen, came to our clubs and activities as well, and she is now a fulltime employee of ours as well.

In 2002, we began to dream of having our own "drop in" for young people on the estate. We had no money, but we had seen God provide miraculously before. We rented a vacant shop on the estate next to our lunch club where many bored young people gather to buy and sell drugs. The cost to redecorate the shop was over £20,000. We started the work and we prayed like mad for

God's provision, and the money began to come. One day a bill came for £3500 that had to be paid within three days.

We couldn't see where we were going to get the money, and young people were getting impatient that we hadn't opened. I explained to the group of youths that we could open when we got the money to finish redecorating the place. Then I told them that we needed £3500 within the next three days, or we were in trouble.

The young people decided that they needed to pray with us, so they prayed out some prayers (amidst giggles) for the cash to come in. Later that night, someone who did not know our need gave a check for £1000. The next day we got a check for another £1000, and the following day we got a further £1500 from some people we'd never met. This is just one example of the times God has been faithful in providing for us when we were obedient to follow the dreams He put in our hearts. It didn't take us long to open what is now called "The Juice Bar."

PAYING THE PRICE

God has been faithful, but this has not all been easy and has come at a cost. Our staff and volunteers have been attacked, had their houses burgled, been robbed on the street, and had their car windows smashed. We've experienced funding cuts, verbal accusations, and had The Juice Bar and lunch club robbed on a number of occasions. But, none of these hardships are significant compared to the great blessing of seeing so many lives changed.

One lad who had taken part in our trips out, activity holidays, football, and music clubs and had been given a mentor, attacked me last Christmas. He had been in trouble with the police and had been excluded from different schools. However over this last year, he began to come to our Bible studies that we started for young people in The Juice Bar. He is now doing better at school, has become a Christian, and got baptized recently.

One Sunday afternoon three and a half years ago, I was sitting in my flat with my wife, Clare, when we saw a helicopter landing outside on the estate. We went out to see what was going on. There were loads of police around, and the helicopter was Air Ambulance. A 15-year-old boy had been stabbed severely where The Juice Bar is now. Some people were saying he had died, while others were saying he was still alive. As we walked around, we prayed that the boy who was called Paul would be saved, that he wouldn't die, and that he would follow Jesus and be used mightily by God.

Paul survived the stabbing, but went on to be one of the bad boys on the estate. He became a drug dealer and lived a life of drugs, sex, and raving. He was one of the tough lads, and because he was one of the best Rap MCs in the area, other youths on the estate admired him and had great respect for him.

Last year, something amazing happened. One night there was a fight about to take place among 12 lads outside the shops. A youth worker was there and was worried, as the lads were the kind of guys that could seriously hurt each other. He began to pray that God would bring His peace into the situation. Three hours later, the lads were all still there, but there had been no fight. The Spirit of God had fallen upon the group, many of whom were notorious for being involved with crime and crack dealing.

It happened that Paul was there that night, and as the group stood outside the shops with their hands held together as they prayed, the lads all experienced something of God. Paul is now following Jesus with everything he has. He now has a consuming passion to help other young people to find Jesus, has read the entire Bible (in ten months), and has been a catalyst for helping others find a personal relationship with Jesus Christ.

Another one of the lads there that night was a 19-year-old who was one of the main drug dealers in a neighboring estate. He carried his own gun and had a bad reputation. He is now also on fire for

God and carries his Bible everywhere, sharing his faith with anyone and everyone.

ABOVE ALL WE COULD ASK OR THINK

Just a little over five years ago it was only a dream to see lives changed and the kingdom of God come to the Alton estate. We still have a long way to go, but we have seen God do amazing things. God has provided for us and enabled us to start many new initiatives and projects on the estate for thousands of residents.

They include twice-weekly trips out to places of interest for isolated elderly, a visiting program to their homes, activities, holidays and parties. For children and young people, God has enabled us to set up mentoring schemes, football clubs, youth club events, music nights, residential holidays, dance clubs, homework clubs, school work help (assemblies, reading support and group mentoring), relationship education, a children's church, a Juice Bar drop in and much more.

Last summer, we organised two weeks of events and activities for the whole community in a huge tent in the middle of the estate. Various known villains got involved with fundraising and helping us throw a party for nearly 500 elderly people, as well as free BBQs and fun days for thousands and loads of activities for all ages—from infants to 95-year-olds. God wants His body on earth to grow and to make the difference that so many people need in their lives.

The original dream with Regenerate.com has been surpassed as God has used us to reach thousands, both young and old, on the estate. We are now dreaming about working with other churches on other estates also. The cell group has now grown into Roehampton Community Church and is steadily growing as we seek to live out church-life on the estate.

In August 2005, the Lord directed us to partner with another church to take a team of young people from the estates to help put on a camp for Street Children and young people from the poverty stricken slums of Nakuru, Kenya. The young people from the estates were blown away by the poverty in Kenya, but also by the openness to God that there is among the Kenyan people. The experience had such an impact on the lives of young people from the Alton Estate (who would never normally get an opportunity like this) that we are going to organize regular trips. This will give more young people the opportunity to make a difference to others who are less fortunate than themselves.

An admonition that we were given when we began Regenerate.com[1] was this, "These are not days to have a small view of God, or to have a small view of what you can do in God, but these are days to look at your mighty God, a God who can do the impossible."

Dare to ask God for big things that are impossible with man. He will not disappoint you.

৪৩ ঌ ৬৫৪

Andy's story challenges us to not only pray for people to be saved and for God's will to be done, but to get out of our boat (our comfort zone) and become fishers of men. Many times God will use you to answer your prayers and you will receive His abundant supply.

chapter 11

RECEIVING FROM THE INVISIBLE SUPPLY

By faith, we see the world was called into
existence by God's word. What we see was
created by what we don't see.

—HEBREWS 11:13
THE MESSAGE

We like comfort zones. God doesn't. Comfort zones don't require anything of us that will help us grow, and they don't require anything from God. God likes a challenge. He is a Creator and enjoys doing new things. So God usually doesn't give us a plan that is fully funded before we step out in faith and obey Him.

Jesus taught, "Do not worry about everyday life—whether you have enough food, drink, and clothes. Why be like the pagans who are so deeply concerned about these things? Your heavenly Father already knows all your needs, and He will give you all you need from day to day, if you live for Him and make the kingdom of God your primary concern" (Matt. 6:25,31-33 NLT).

Seeking His kingdom first and His righteousness puts us in touch with God's miraculous supply. If we make seeking our provision our first priority, then we don't qualify as candidates for the miraculous. We have taken things into our own hands, and now we will have to trust in ourselves and rely on the world's way of getting our provision.

When Jesus sent out His twelve disciples and then later sent out seventy-two other believers to preach about the coming of the kingdom of God and to heal the sick, He instructed them, "Don't even take along a walking stick, nor a traveler's bag, nor food, nor money. Not even an extra coat." Later, He asked, "When I sent you out to preach, did you lack anything?" They said, "Nothing!" (Luke 9:3,10:4,22:35 NLT). As they stepped out in faith and obeyed Him, God provided all their needs.

MIRACLE MONEY

One year, my family was holding a youth conference in Mexico. Here I met one of my favorite people, Anna Mendez—an evangelist who was in charge of the conference. I will never forget all the stories she told us about her life and living by faith. I had never heard such amazing faith-building stories. One of the stories she shared was about a wallet she had that never ran out of money.

The Lord had told her to give away all her earthly possessions and to live by faith and preach the Gospel. One day after she had been preaching the Gospel for a while, she wanted to give an offering to the Lord, but she had nothing to give. She asked the Lord to put ten pesos in her wallet so she would have something to give. At this time, she thought that ten pesos was a great amount of money.

The next time she opened her wallet, there were the ten pesos she had prayed for. Believe it or not, those ten pesos kept reappearing in her wallet, even after she had given the offering. God told her to use the money for what she needed, and it kept coming. Every time she pulled out the ten pesos to use for her needs, ten more would appear in her wallet.

She explained that the next time she wanted to increase her faith, she prayed for 100 pesos to appear in her wallet, so she could give a bigger offering to the Lord. This would be the biggest offering she had ever given. The same situation happened again. A hundred pesos miraculously appeared in her wallet, which she immediately put in the offering.

Every time she opened her wallet 100 pesos would be there to meet her needs. This is how God took care of her and her expenses, ministry, conferences, and everything else. The last time I saw her, she had asked the Lord to enable her to give an offering of 100,000 pesos, and God had provided for the offering as well as for her needs. The Lord no longer provides her needs through the wallet, but she is praying that she will be able to give the Lord a million pesos.

I am sharing this with you, so you will not limit the way God provides for you. Maybe you are thinking that a miracle like this one that happened to the lady in Mexico could never happen for you. Well actually, when she told us this story my mom and I looked at each other with a funny look because we both remembered a wallet I used to have when I was younger.

I still remember everything about that wallet. I always asked my mom how I got the money that I found inside. There were always big bills in it that my parents never put there. When the evangelist shared this story, both my mother and I understood what had happened with my wallet. You may be asking, "Wow! Do you still have that wallet?" I only can say, I wish I did. One day I realized I had lost my wallet, and I have never found it since. The Lord, however, supplies in other ways.

When I was little, I had a poster over my bed that was a picture of a little girl who had a wagon full of puppies that she was trying to give away. Under the picture was the inscription, "God Loves a Cheerful Giver." That statement was honestly the motto of my childhood. I found my joy in giving everything away and saving up my money to buy people gifts. I always loved to give offerings in church. This is why I know I had that wallet with endless money as a child.

Recently, I was laying in bed trying to fall asleep, when I felt God begin to speak to me. When the Lord speaks to you, it is not usually an audible voice—it is a tug on your heart, and then you hear a sweet soft voice that you know is His voice. He began to speak to me about faith and money. He said, "Evangeline, do you know why I reward those who give?" It seems that before Jesus teaches you something, He always asks you a question first to get you to think about it.

"I think I know," I answered. Then I started giving the Lord different explanations. After I had given my ideas, Jesus said, "Well, if people have a hard time giving up money, it's because they are putting their faith in money instead of Me. They think that if they give their money, then they will not have provision, and that there is no way to receive more. Their faith is in the money to provide, instead of in Me. I own the cattle on a thousand hills and can do any miracle needed to make provision necessary."

How do we show God that we have faith in Him for our supply? Faith is shown by saying, "I trust in You Lord." Faith is trusting in the Giver, not the gift.

My sister, Stephanie, who now lives in Switzerland, told me a story about God's miraculous provision. One of her friends was looking at apartments for rent. She couldn't afford much, so she was thinking she could get a roommate and get a nicer apartment. God told her, "I don't want you to have a roommate, and I want you to get the nicest apartment—I will provide!" So she believed God and made arrangements to rent the nicest apartment she could find. At this time she did not know how she was going to pay the rent.

A few days later, she went down into her basement to look for something and opened up a closet that she had never looked in before. There lying on the floor was the exact amount of money that she needed to rent the new apartment that God wanted to bless her with. However, if she hadn't stepped out in faith and gotten the apartment, she wouldn't have needed God's miraculous supply!

FAITH IN GOD'S PROVISION

God rewards our faith and our obedience. Jesus always healed people once they stepped out in faith to believe. Their faith made them well. It is the same way with finances. Our faith brings our provision. Too often we look at the natural circumstances and limit how God will do the things He promises. He doesn't work the way we think He should work.

Not only will He use other believers to meet your needs, He can send angels to provide money for you, or multiply money in your account, or set up the divine appointments you need. Whatever your need, He cares about it and wants to provide for you. David reminds us, "Those who trust in the Lord will not lack any good thing" (Ps. 34:10).

I graduated from high school in 2002, and right after graduation I moved to Seattle, Washington, for an internship program at the City Church in Kirkland, Washington. Even though my dad provided for me and supported me at that time, he always wanted to see how much money I could believe God for, so I could learn to live by faith.

I had saved up some money from working to pay for some of the things I was going to need when I moved to Seattle. I also sent support letters out for the internship program to a lot of my friends and to some of my parent's friends as well. One of my dad's friend's that I sent my support letter to was Dr. David Yongi Cho, the pastor of one of the largest churches in the world in Seoul, Korea.

During this time, my sister Stephanie and her husband were visiting us. My sister had gone to the dentist and received a report that she needed to get a lot of dental work done. She was very upset because of the high cost of this work. I felt the Lord instruct me to give her $250 of my savings from working to put towards her dental bill. I put the money in an envelope and secretly placed it in her drawer, eagerly waiting for her to find the money. Of course, when she found it, she knew it was from me. She tried to give it back to me, but I kept telling her not to rob me of my blessing and to keep it.

Over dinner that evening, my family was talking about the letters I had sent out to people. The letter that my family found very presumptuous was the one I had sent to Dr. Cho. They felt that a pastor with over a million people in his church would get letters like that all the time, and they were sure that he was so busy he wouldn't even have the opportunity to read my letter. Well, I just told them that I felt led to send him one for some reason. Right after dinner the phone rang, so I ran to get it. It was my dad's secretary calling.

"Evangeline," she said, "I have good news for you. A fax just came in from Seoul, Korea from a man named Dr. Yongi Cho. He said he was praying this morning, and he feels that the Lord wants him to give you $500 for your internship in Seattle. He also wrote you a full-page letter." I was so blessed and I realized that this gift was an immediate double return from the money I gave to my sister. I think that God wanted to show me that nothing is too big for Him. Needless to say, my whole family was amazed.

Recently, I was going to Tennessee to see my brother. Before the plane was boarding I had a little time, so I thought I would get a smoothie at the shop next to my gate. They gave me the smoothie, and as I was standing their drinking it, they informed me that I couldn't pay with my check card. My gate was still not boarding, so I ran to the ATM to get the money. When I got back to my gate, I had missed my boarding time, and the gate was closed!

I started panicking. I asked the ticket agents, "What am I supposed to do?" They told me I could wait for five or six hours until the next flight. I was so upset. I asked, "Can't you make the plane turn around and get me?" Of course this was a stupid question. They wouldn't even look at me, or help me. I then realized this was not something I could work out. God had to work this out, so I said, "Grace, Grace," which means, "God not in my strength, but in Yours."

Suddenly, the little red phone at the gate rang and the pilot said, "Is there anyone out there wanting to get on the plane?"

They whispered in the phone, "Yes, a young lady is out here."

The pilot told her, "Well, bring her to the plane."

Eyeing me with a look of scorn, the ticket agent asked her co-worker, "Should we let her on?"

"Of course!" her co-worker responded.

Quickly, they opened the gate and took me to the plane. I was so nervous from almost missing my plane that I was still shaking when I sat down in my seat and realized what God had done for me!

You might say, that it wasn't such a big deal that you missed your plane. No, it wasn't really a big deal. I could have waited for the next plane, but God cares so much about all of our needs that He provided the way for me to catch my flight and not have to wait for five hours for the next plane.

GOD SUPPLIES EVERY NEED

A number of years before I met Anna Mendez, the evangelist from Mexico, she had been asked to be one of the translators for a prominent U. S. evangelist who was holding a crusade in Mexico City. She declined and explained that she barely knew any English and wouldn't possibly be able to do it.

The morning of the crusade, the director called Anna and said that they could find no one else to translate for the crusade. She again explained that she did not have an adequate knowledge of English to make the translation. The crusade director told her, "Well, the Lord told me you were supposed to be the translator, so you will just have to trust Him to help you." Anna prayed and said, "Okay, Lord, I will obey You, and if I look like a fool, then I guess I will be one."

The night of the meeting, with fear and trembling, she somehow walked onto the platform. She knew that if the Lord didn't come through, the evangelist's whole meeting that so many people had spent so much time putting together would be ruined. The evangelist gave a few words of greeting. She knew enough English to give some sort of Spanish translation.

As the speaker launched into his sermon, Anna's knees began to shake. She prayed, "O Lord, don't fail me now." She stepped out in faith and began to translate the English words into Spanish, and suddenly the Lord gave her the understanding of the whole English language. Anna was able to not only interpret that message, but was also able to understand English and speak it fluently and read it from that day on.

My parents told me a similar story about one of the missionaries they sent to Argentina who was trying very hard to learn Spanish. An evangelist came down to help the missionary and said, "This is ridiculous. If you are going to be effective here to reach leaders you need to speak Spanish fluently." He called the missionary forward in the meeting and laid hands on him for the gift of Spanish. From that day on he could read, speak, and write Spanish, so much so that everyone there thought he was a native Argentinean. I believe that this miracle will happen for me some day when I need it.

Some People said It Could Never be Done

Consider what people have said would never happen, yet a dreamer with a dream called the impossible, possible, and saw that which existed only in the invisible realms become a reality through his imagination.[1]

- "A rocket will never be able to leave the earth's atmosphere."
  - *The New York Times, 1936*

- "The atomic bomb will never go off— and I speak as an expert in explosives."
  -*U.S. Admiral William Leahy in 1945*

- "I have traveled the length and breadth of this country and talked with the best people, and I can assure you that data processing is a fad that won't last out the year."
  -*The editor in charge of business books for Prentice Hall, 1957.*

- So we went to Atari and said, "Hey, we've got this amazing thing—even built with some of your parts— what do you think about funding us? Or we'll give it to you. We just want to do it. Pay our salary, we'll come work for you." And they said, "No." So then we went to Hewlett-Packard who said, "Hey, we don't need you. You haven't finished college yet."
  -*Apple Computer Inc. founder Steve Jobs on attempts to get Atari and H-P interested in his and Steve Wozniak's personal computer.*

- "Drill for oil? You mean drill into the ground to try and find oil? You're crazy!"
  -*Drillers who Edwin L. Drake tried to enlist to his project to drill for oil in 1859.*

- "Well-informed people know it is impossible to transmit the voice over wires and that were it possible to do so, the thing would be of no practical value."
  -*Boston Post, 1865.*

- "The concept is interesting and well-formed, but in order to earn better than a 'C,' the idea must be feasible."
  -A Yale University professor in response to Fred Smith's paper proposing reliable overnight delivery service. Smith ignored him and went on to found Federal Express.

- "That rainbow song's no good. Take it out."
  -MGM memo after first showing of "The Wizard Of Oz." "Somewhere Over the Rainbow" went on to become an all-time classic.

- "Forget it. No Civil War picture ever made a nickel."
  -MGM executive, advising against investing in Gone With The Wind.

- "Louis Pasteur's theory of germs is ridiculous fiction."
  -Pierre Pachet, Professor of Physiology at Toulouse, 1872. Pasteur ignored him and continued developing his theory. As the result of Pasteur's work on the germ theory, Joseph Lister realized that germs were causing many people to die in the hospital and began the use of antiseptics in Surgery.

- "I think there is a world market for maybe five computers."
  -IBM chairman Thomas Watson

- "The wireless music box has no imaginable commercial value. Who would pay for a message sent to nobody in particular?"
  -David Sarnoff's associates in response to his urgings for investment in the radio in the 1920s.

- "Airplanes are interesting toys but of no military value."
  -Marechal Ferdinand Foch, Professor of Strategy, Ecole Superieure de Guerre.

- "Can't act. Can't sing. Slightly bald. Can dance a little."
  -A film company's verdict on Fred Astaire's 1928 screen test.

- "You ain't going nowhere, son. You ought to go back to driving a truck."
  -The Grand Ole Opry's Jim Denny to Elvis Presley, 1954.

- "How does it feel to have failed seven hundred times?" The man responded, "I have not failed seven hundred times. I have not failed once. I have succeeded in proving that those seven hundred ways will not work. When I have eliminated the ways that will *not* work, I will find the way that *will* work."
  -A New York Times reporter to Thomas Edison after seven hundred unsuccessful attempts to invent the electric light. Several thousand more of these failure/ successes followed, but Edison finally found the one that would work, and invented the electric light bulb.[2]

chapter 12

SUPERNATURAL PROVISION

The difference between being involved and being committed
can be seen in a ham and egg breakfast. The chicken was
involved—the pig was committed.

—ANONYMOUS

Dear brothers and sisters, what's the use of saying you have
faith if you don't prove it by your actions? Faith that doesn't
show itself by good deeds is no faith at all—is dead and
useless.

—JAMES 2:14,17

This is a story about Tilo Reichold. Ten years ago God called Tilo
and his wife Cathleen, to step out in faith and start a Christian youth
church in Germany they called, "Die Arche,"[1] which means The
Ark. Tilo tells of how God's supernatural provision manifested
every time they took a new step of faith.

TILO'S STORY

I grew up in the former DDR (Deutsche Democratic Republic,
Eastern Germany when it was part of the Soviet Bloc). As a young
man, I completed a degree in music as a singer, and as my occupa-
tion, I was a singer with a band for many years after. I traveled with

a rock music-group throughout the whole country. However, my personal life went more and more downhill as I allowed sin to dominate my life. I became involved in many things that had many negative influences, and I took drugs and drank too much.

When I was 26-years-old, I was at the lowest point of my life. At this time, I found Jesus. He gave me a new life and a new vision to live for—and for me, it truly was literally like a new life began.

A NEW LIFE

This passion for Jesus and the new life I had gave me a new perspective and zeal for living. It motivated me to invest my time to help teenagers, the ones that were living on the crooked path. The youth in this nation are in a bad state. Life among young people here in Germany is characterized by resignation and hopelessness. Less than five percent of the young people here have a connection to church or the Christian faith. Instead, they are connected to occultism, Satanism, and left-wing radicalism is booming. Drug addiction and violence are getting to be big problems in our schools.

In the residential-area in our city, I saw increasingly more and more young people who lacked a good perspective on life—children who already smoked, and teenagers who drank and did drugs regularly. Helping these young people began to become a big concern of mine.

When I saw these problems I began to pray: "God, how can I help them?" After a short time, God gave me the vision to start a Christian youth-church. With some Christian friends from Chemnitz (our town) and the surrounding area, we founded the youth-church, Die Arche (The Ark) in 1995. It was our vision that there must be a radical place where young people who would never go to a church could find Jesus. We kept our hearts surrendered to the Lord and prayed and put all our money together in order to get a building for a Christian youth center.

We now have more than 60 volunteers who commit themselves to talk to the young people about Jesus at the outreaches as well as do follow-up. In addition, the Die Arche team organizes evangelistic youth meetings in churches, youth clubs, or events like the Chemnitz Town Festival, where more than 1,000 people came to the stage of Die Arche to hear about Jesus.

The most important part of our project is the weekly "Jesus-Party," which is an evangelistic service for young people who are not yet saved. In the past few years, a lot of young people have received Jesus during these services. Among these young people were Satanists, criminals, and drug addicts. Now, many of these who were saved are a part of our team and are sharing their story to bring others to the knowledge of the truth. God hasn't given up on this so-called lost generation. His heart beats for those who are furthest away from Him. He gives new hope to this generation.

How Everything Started

In 1998, during a time of prayer, the Lord spoke to us in a very unusual way. We felt God leading us to buy the former cinema "Weltecho" for a new youth center. After seriously asking ourselves whether we had gone mad, we started to pursue this idea. The owner of the cinema told us the price was one million DM. (Note: DM or German marks are no longer in use. This would equal 510,000 euros, or $694,000). For a small organization like ours with monthly donations of less than 1,000 DM, this sounded crazy, but in the following two-years God began to show us that it was His will that we purchase this property.

In the year 2000, we began to negotiate the price with the owner of the cinema. To our surprise, we were offered the building for only 350,000 DM. This was a huge answer to prayer. We agreed to this price and said that we would have the money to him in the next few weeks. At this point, we had no money and were going to attempt to get it through a loan. A few days later the owner told us there would be another investor who could pay the money immediately. That meant that our business deal was off.

We didn't know what to think about this situation. After intensive prayer with all our leaders, we felt that God was challenging us to trust that He would provide the money, not the bank. Trusting in God, we phoned the owner once again and told him that we were ready to sign the contract right away because we had secured the financing (because we knew that God would do it).

We were told to come to the notary's office in three days time to sign the contract and to bring the deposit of 55,000 DM with us. At that time, we only had 7,000 DM in our bank account, but we realised that there was no turning back, so we confirmed that we would have it there. Right after we confirmed the deal, we all looked at each other and knew that only a miracle could help us.

MIRACLES REALLY DO HAPPEN

Only a few minutes later the doorbell rang. A young man came into our office and told us that he felt he was supposed to stop by. After telling him about our present situation he replied, "Now I see why I'm here—I will give you 10,000 DM." This was all of his savings. This was the first and, at the same time, the biggest single donation we had received for the "Weltecho" purchase. It was simply a miracle. After the young man had left, we fell down on our knees and repented for our lack of faith.

From this point on, the miracles didn't stop. We certainly will never forget the following two days. Starting early in the morning until late at night, there was a constant coming and going of Christians who were bringing donations. Within four days, over 100 Christians donated so much money that we not only had the needed deposit, we had more than 85,000 DM! God really worked a miracle. However, we still had to raise another 300,000 DM within

8 weeks. One could really write a book about all the things that happened during this time. Christians of all denominations became one in favor of this project.

There was spontaneous fund-raising in churches, among friends, and even in companies. The Lord touched many hearts in a very special way. An old lady who had a very low pension phoned and told us she would donate 50 DM. She was sorry that she couldn't give more. A short time later she called again. She had thought about it and decided that she had enough to eat so she could give another 10 DM. An 8-year-old boy who was saving up for a new football brought us all his savings.

A homeless man who visited our programs collected scrap metal and brought that to the scrap dealer. He brought us the money he received—21 DM. A child collected money from his friends and gave us 11.20 DM. We could tell a lot of other similar stories. It is an absolute miracle how God touches hearts. After these 8 weeks, more than 700 people had donated more than 400,000 DM!

GOD IS BUILDING A HOME FOR THE LOST

In the spring of 2000, we had the first big work party at the "Weltecho." The first person who came to help was a young homeless man who had visited our events. He said, "God has spoken to me last night, 'Go to the Weltecho and help them tomorrow morning'—and here I am." This touched us deeply and showed us that for God it is not about the external building project, that He doesn't want to renovate ruined buildings—He wants to heal broken hearts. This is the only reason why God is building this house. It is to become a center of the healing love of God, which the young people need so desperately.

In May 2000, the renovation work started. This building was over 100-years-old and was completely run down. First, the house had to be gutted. This alone filled more than 100 containers with rubble. The roof couldn't be saved and had to be completely removed, as well as the floors, ceilings, and major parts of the walls. During the work it turned out that the renovation of the whole building would cost at least 1.5 million DM, even if we did a lot of the work ourselves. This was another challenge in faith. How could it be possible to raise so much money once again after most of our friends had given the last of their money?

We had been experiencing again and again how God works miracles, but on the other hand this was a huge challenge. This challenge pushed us to our limits. Up until this point, we had been financing the building works through small donations from our friends, and most of the donators were the young people themselves who came to our programs. They sometimes gave money, which they barely could spare.

To this date, through a lot of miracles, we have been able to complete the outside of the building. We have been able to roof the building, to install new windows, and to do most of the work on sanitation and electricity, too. In the past two years, more than 100 different people have worked voluntarily on the building site so that we could do almost all of the necessary work on our own.

Today, we can say that we've gotten through the major part of the work. By the time this book is published we will probably be finished with the construction. But one thing we are sure of, with God's help, we will come to the end of this project and complete the renovation as planned. Ultimately we know that this is not about the building—it is about the young people themselves for whom God is building this house.

ഇൗ ൂ෴ ฝ ശ

Tilo's burden for the lost caused him to step out in faith to receive God's supernatural supply to see lives touched and changed by the power of God. If you don't have a burden to reach the world for Jesus Christ, ask Jesus to give you one. Then step out and do His will. God's provision will be manifested through your obedience and your faith will soar.

chapter 13

THE POWER OF YOUR THOUGHTS

What our free will is meant to do is to
help God write the story.

—MADELINE L'ENGLE

WALKING ON WATER

By faith, the impossible becomes a reality. By faith, we bring things from the invisible realm into the visible realm. But practically, how do we get those things that exist in the realm of the spirit and the dream to appear in the natural?

Let's consider what faith really is. The Bible tells us that faith is "the confident assurance that what we hope for is going to happen" (Heb. 11:1 NLT). It is important to understand that your faith is not what you say you believe. Your real beliefs are the actual thoughts that you meditate on and hold in your mind.

You don't have faith if you say that you believe one thing, and then entertain doubts as to whether you really believe it is true in your heart. "With the heart, man believes unto righteousness" (Rom. 10:10). It is in your heart, which is simply the thoughts of your mind, that you either agree with God's Word or you entertain the devil's doubts.

Paul tells us where our spiritual battle really lies: "For the weapons of our warfare are not carnal but mighty in God for pulling down strongholds, casting down arguments and every high thing that exalts itself against the knowledge of God, bringing every thought into captivity to the obedience of Christ" (2 Cor. 10:4-5).

THE BATTLE FOR YOUR MIND

There is a battle going on for your mind. Why? Because your mind is like a bed of rich soil that has the power to cause all kinds of seeds to grow and bring forth fruit, whether good or bad. The enemy wants to plant his seeds there, and God wants to plant His seeds of Truth and Light. The seeds that are actually planted in the rich soil of your mind are the thoughts you entertain, rehearse, meditate and dwell upon, and they have a promise of bringing a harvest of whatever has been planted. A world lies in the harvest of a seed. Consider the giant oak tree that grows from a small acorn. Can a fig seed grow olives? Can you gather grapes from thorns?

What you think and meditate on determines what your life will produce. Solomon explains that the most important events in your life comes out of your hearts' meditation: "Keep your heart with all diligence, for out of it spring the issues of life" (Prov. 4:23). The exciting thing is that you have the power to decide what seeds are planted in your heart. You have the power to choose what you think upon. The devil wants to use your meditations to disrupt God's plan. God wants to use your meditations to bring His will to pass. Agree with God, not the devil.

Because Adam and Eve listened to Satan and agreed with the lies that he told and acted on them, the human race fell into sin. Paul emphasizes the importance of guarding our heart and tells us, "Take every thought captive to the obedience of Christ." To be effective in the greatest way for Christ's kingdom, you must cast down every thought and argument that contradicts the Word of God, plead the blood of Jesus over your mind, let the Word of

God and His promises fill your mind richly, and meditate continually upon all that is good and true.

The Bible reminds us that, "As a man thinks in his heart so is he" (Prov. 23:7). What is our heart? In *Strong's Concordance*, we learn that the Greek word for "heart" in every New Testament passage except two comes from the Greek word *kardia* from the primary root *kar* meaning "the heart," and figuratively signifies, "the thoughts and feelings of the mind."[1] Jesus commands us, "Love the Lord with all your heart (thoughts and feelings), mind, and strength." Paul explains that, "with the heart (thoughts and feelings) man believes unto righteousness" (Rom. 10:8a).

YOUR FAITH—YOUR THOUGHTS

Your faith then is the belief of your mind, and the belief of your mind is the thoughts and feelings that you hold in your mind and think on everyday. You can increase your faith by simply changing your thoughts and feelings. Hold God's Word and His promises in your thoughts. Whatever you think on today is what you are believing for. What you allow yourself to think and meditate on today, whether good or bad, will determine what you bring into your future.

This truth of the power of your thoughts can be seen even in a simple thing like having a good day or a bad day. If you spend time *thinking* of all the bad things that have happened to you during the day and *feeling* bad about the lousy time you are having, it is most likely you will continue to have a terrible day. Yet, if you choose to meditate only on the good things of that day and dwell on feelings of joy and well being, it is most likely you will have a good day.

You can always be thankful for something—for being able to talk, walk, breathe, function as a human being, for friends and fellowship, for family, for the food you eat, for the freedom you have to trust God in your heart and pray to Him. Remember, your thoughts are seeds being planted in the garden of your mind, and they will bring forth fruit in your life for good or evil.

Ask yourself this question: are you a person who sees the cup half empty or half full? The thoughts you choose will determine the kind of life that you live. Jesus wants to pour out His blessings on those with "a joyful heart"—"a thankful heart."

Throughout scripture we see how God blesses the thankful. Consider this verse: "Because you did not serve the Lord your God with joy and a glad heart for the abundance of all things; therefore you shall serve your enemies who the Lord will send against you, in hunger, in thirst, in nakedness, and in lack of all things, and He will put an iron yoke on your neck until He has destroyed you" (Deut. 28:47-48).

Many people blame the devil for their problems when they need to draw a circle around themselves and then look inside it to find out the true cause of their misery. According to this passage, if you continue to be an unthankful person, God himself will send an iron yoke of destruction against you. This is the reason why many Christians live weak and defeated lives. If this is you, you can repent right now and start being thankful for everything God has given you. Turn away from all negative, depressing thoughts and make your thoughts joyful. "God's promises are always yes and amen" (2 Cor. 1:20a).

If you are one of those people who always sees the cup half empty instead of half full, then you need to begin to change the way you think. Make a list of all the things you are thankful for. You will be shocked at the way your life, and even your attitude, will change when you change your thinking process. Paul exhorts the believers, "Be transformed by the renewing of your mind" (Heb. 11:3).

THE PIPELINE

Dr. Robert Schuller once explained that the most significant revelation he ever received on faith was to understand that faith is a pipeline through which we bring the blessings of God—His will, His power, and His purposes—from the invisible realm to the visible realm. Faith is the way we release God's blessings and His miracle power on the earth. Dr. Schuller explained that faith is not a quality we are trying to get, because everyone has already been given *a measure of faith* (Rom.12:3b).

The fact that each of us has a measure of faith is evident from the daily activities of life. When we are sleeping, we believe we will wake up; when we are flying, we believe we will get to our destination; when we sit in a chair, we believe it will not break. I am sure that you can think of hundreds of things that you do on a daily basis that in some way is an exercise of faith.

Dr. Schuller likened faith to a satellite dish. The satellite dish does nothing on its own. It is an instrument that we use to bring a picture or information into our house. The satellite dish doesn't decide the picture or information we receive, we are the ones that are holding the control and determine which channel we will tune in.

We can either bring in something good and edifying into our home, or we can choose to look at filth or some negative image. We alone have the power to turn the channel. The question is, what thoughts and ideas are you bringing into your heart through the remote control of your faith? What are you looking at? What thoughts are you holding in your mind? This is the determining factor of what your faith will produce. [2]

STANDING ON GOD'S PROMISES

The measure of faith that God has given to you will bring the thoughts that you hold in your mind from the invisible into the visible. Faith that is focusing on the Word of God says, "Regardless of the circumstances I see in front of me, I am going to stand on the word that God has spoken to me." Looking at your current circumstances will never activate faith in God's Word. Almost always, circumstances will make God's promise seem impossible.

Think about how impossible it is was for Sarah, a 90-year-old woman, to give birth, for Noah to build an ark for a flood when at that time no one had even seen rain before, and for Joseph to finally become a ruler in Egypt when his circumstances had confined him to a lifetime of slavery. Moses had faith that Pharaoh would let the people go regardless of the impossible circumstances he faced, and by faith he would later stand in front of the Red Sea and see the waters part to make a way for the Israelites to escape because God had promised.

Miriam, Joshua, Caleb, Gideon, Samson, David, and a host of others also had to face impossible circumstances to do the will of God, armed with faith in God's promises alone. Countless saints down through the ages have stood in faith on the promises of God and have seen their circumstances changed and the world reborn. The young people whose stories are retold in this book have seen God's mighty power because they believed that God would do what He promised.

Jesus is looking for people who have faith in Him and in His promises. While Jesus was on earth, although He was God in the flesh, in some cities He could do nothing because of their unbelief. To the woman with the issue of blood Jesus said, "Your faith has made you well" (Matt. 9:22). Jesus asked this profound question: "When the Son of Man comes, will He find faith on the earth?"(Luke 18:18). Ultimately, whether you are a person of "great faith in God" or not will be determined by the opinion you hold of the One who has made the promises.

THE POWER OF BELIEVING

J.W. Redfield, a Methodist minister in the early part of the 20th century, spent years seeking to be sanctified and baptized in the love of God. He finally realized that it was a matter of simply believing. Redfield wrote about this revelation: "I saw the way of faith as never before. I said, 'Lord, I have tried everything I honestly know to do, but faith. Now, I will to trust in You.' And I learned that in Jesus dwells all the fullness of the Godhead bodily. Jesus said, 'Ask and you will receive so your joy may be full.' I now felt the power of those words as never before. It seemed no risk to hang a world's salvation on the merits of Christ. I asked and I received. In this light, I saw the sin of unbelief to be the great soul-destroying sin of the world, and in comparison to it murder, robbery, and other sins were of small account."[3]

How could this minister compare unbelief to such terrible sins? God has promised to forgive you for every sin, but you cannot receive that forgiveness and salvation unless you believe. Therefore, unbelief is the sin that will ultimately destroy your soul and keep you out of God's kingdom. Unless you agree with God and His Word, and through your faith, act on it, He can do absolutely nothing for you or through you. His will and purposes for you will not be accomplished in the earth, and your work in this world for the kingdom of God will be aborted.

CREATED TO BE A CREATOR

Another way to understand faith is to realize just how man is created in the image of God. At the beginning of creation, everything God made existed first in His thoughts. God had specific designs, colors, shapes and purposes for everything He was going to create. The Spirit of God was brooding over the face of the waters and the earth was without form and void. Then God—having envisioned what He would create—said, "Let there be"—and there was!

God formed mankind in His image with the power to create—He gave everyone the ability to create anything by brooding over it through his or her imagination. This God-given power to create was evident in the early years of man's history. Unfortunately, men and women used their God given power of imagination to create bad things.

In fact, God told Noah that he was going to destroy the earth with a flood because of the misuse of this creative power. The deciding factor—"God saw that the wickedness of man was great in the earth, and that *every imagination of the thoughts of his heart was only evil continually*" (Gen. 6:5). After the flood at the building of the tower of Babel, God confused men's language and scattered them because He said, "Now nothing will be restrained from them, which they have *imagined* to do" (Gen. 11:6).

Dr. David Yongi Cho, pastor of the largest church in the world in Seoul, Korea refers to this creative ability in every person, in his book *The Fourth Dimension*. He explains that thoughts are like eggs, and through your imagination, you are like a hen brooding over the nest to hatch her chicks. If you meditate and brood over toxic eggs (negative thoughts) you will hatch a bunch of toxic chickens (events).

Brooding over negative thoughts and attaching strong emotion to it will cause you to bring forth that which is opposite from the will of God. Dr. Cho cautions that you should choose your thoughts wisely. Your mind has the power to bring your meditations to birth, creating your reality.[4]

James confirms this idea: "Each one is tempted when he is drawn away by his own desires and enticed. Then, when desire has conceived, it gives birth to sin and when sin is full grown it brings forth death" (James 1:14-15). Jesus always emphasized the heart (thoughts) as the place of the birth of sin. "Lust in the heart" (thoughts) is adultery; "anger in the heart" (thoughts) is the same thing as murder. Jesus also emphasized the heart (thoughts) as the place where miracles are born: "If you say unto this mountain be removed and be cast into the sea and do not doubt in your heart (thoughts), it shall be done." The thoughts of the heart is where the reign of "self" must end. Submit to the reign of Christ and let Christ live and reign in your heart and mind.

As a testimony to the power of imagination and the need to be specific in prayer, Dr. Cho tells that he was praying for a bike, desk, and chair. He said that he prayed and prayed for the bike, desk and chair, but he never got them. Finally, he asked the Lord why he wasn't getting the things that he prayed for since he was praying in faith and needed these things to help him do God's work?

The Lord told him to be more specific and say what kind of desk, chair, and bike he wanted. He thought about the exact models that he wanted and told the Lord, "Okay I want an American bike that is red with speeds, I want a desk that is mahogany, and a big leather chair that I can feel like a big shot in and spin around."[5]

And God did it! Everything he asked for, he received exactly as he envisioned each item! In this, God showed him the importance of meditating on the exact image of the desired object to see it come to manifestation.

An important thing to realize is that the creative power of your imagination is working right now, whether you believe it or not. Your mind will create in accordance with the nature of your thoughts. This is part of the creative process and the way God designed it. If you think good, good will follow, but if you think evil, evil will follow. All this will be done by simply meditating upon it. Look around and see if what you have in your life is not a product of your thoughts. David prayed, "Let the words of my mouth and the meditation of my heart be acceptable in Your sight, O Lord, my strength and my Redeemer" (Ps. 19:14).

HOW TO USE YOUR IMAGINATION

What are you believing for? Let your faith—the thoughts of your mind—become His pipeline for bringing His will to pass on earth as it is in heaven. Spend time in God's Presence and let His Spirit fill you with the pictures and dreams of His divine purpose. Follow Jesus' example when He said, "The Son can do nothing of Himself, He does only what He sees the Father doing. Whatever the Father does, the Son does also" (John 5:19). Use your faith to bring forth God's ideas. Use the imagination that God has given you to agree with God so that you can bring His will to pass in the earth and can bring His power from the invisible realm into the visible.

Write down the visions and plans for your life that God has revealed to you. Your thoughts are made real and alive with strong emotion. Get a vivid picture and attach emotion to it—feel the joy and delight of having received the promise. This becomes your belief—your faith. Leave the "how to" with God.

When you are writing down your God-given vision, don't think of any limitations. If you had all the money in the world, if you could do anything you wanted to do, what would it be? This is what you should write down—not an altered version because you don't see any way your vision could become reality. Then state what you are believing for. Cast out every argument and every vain thought that contradicts God's Word and His promises.

Continue to brood over the vision. Meditate on the fulfillment of the dream just as a hen sits on its nest—she does not quit or give up until the chickens are hatched. Jesus taught that we should pray always and never give up, and we will receive what we asked for. Thank the Lord that you are receiving it, and so it will be done. God will orchestrate everything in the invisible realm to bring it to birth.

How is a baby knit together in the womb of its mother? God does it, and He brings it to birth when it is ready. All the parents have to do is conceive the child and give the mother proper nutrition. Your proper nutrition is feasting on the Bread of Life—God's Presence and His Word. "Let the Word of God dwell in you richly" (Cols. 3:16).

APPLYING YOUR FAITH

I heard Kenneth Copeland explain this kind of faith when the Lord told him to believe for a private jet to fly overseas to preach the Gospel. The Lord had spoken both to Brother Copeland and his wife about believing for this plane. He was putting his faith towards it. How would he do this? He explained that he would close his eyes and think about the plane—he would see himself getting on the plane and flying the plane across the ocean. Then he would picture himself getting out of the plane and walking across the tarmac.

He would feel the breeze and smell the smells. He would see himself going to the auditorium to preach the Gospel to packed crowds, then he would see himself getting back on the plane and flying across the ocean to his home. This is what Brother Copeland called "putting his faith to it." He said that he wasn't going to figure out *how* he could get the money for this plane, or *when* he could get this plane. He was trusting the Lord and using his God-given imagination to agree with God to see the blessing come to pass. He was thanking God for it everyday as though he already had it.

Two years later Brother Copeland sent out an announcement to his supporters to let them know that his plane was here! On the front of the brochure was a picture of him standing with the plane and signing the contract for it. Inside the announcement, the verse was written, "Trust in the Lord and He will make you ride on the high places of the earth!" (Deut. 32:13).

Jesus said, "The Truth is, anyone who believes in Me will do the same works I have done, and even greater works, because I am going to be with the Father. You can ask for anything in My name and I will do it, so that the Son can bring glory to the Father. Yes, ask anything in My name and I will do it!" (John 14:12-14 NLT). "If you abide in Me, and My words abide in you, ask what you desire and it shall be done for you. By this My Father is glorified, that you bear much fruit, and so you are My disciples" (John 15:7). "Until now you have asked nothing in My name. Ask, and you will receive, that your joy may be full" (John 16:24).

BELIEVING FOR THE IMPOSSIBLE

If your image of what you want to do with your life is only something that you believe that you have the ability to do, then you are not applying Biblical faith. The purpose of faith, said Dr. Cho, is to bring miracles to pass and to bring God's power on the scene because He wants to save people. Faith is standing before the Red Sea and seeing it part and the Israelites cross over on dry land— before any of it actually takes place.

The author of Hebrews asks, "What is faith? It is the confident assurance that what we hope for is going to happen. It is the evidence of things we cannot see"(Heb.11:1 NLT). Not only that, when we have faith we find favor with God. We are told in scripture, "God gave approval to people in days of old because of their faith" (Heb. 11:2 NLT).

I have seen a picture of the things I feel the Lord wants me to do with my life. I first saw this picture when I was five-years-old, and I have seen it ever since. God adds things into my picture, and I can see the events taking place, and I can feel what's going on in my vision. In my imagination, I watch the future unfold as in a movie.

The Discovery Channel featured a program about going to Mars and man's desire for interplanetary travel and the history of invention in the world. At the end of it the narrator remarked, "Today's fantasies are tomorrow's facts. If we really want to travel to other planets, we better get busy dreaming." Walt Disney said, "If you can dream it, you can do it." [6]

SUPERNATURAL DIRECTION

One day Oral Roberts was praying for a long time in tongues when God gave him the interpretation and told him to build a university. Oral Roberts told the Lord that he had no money, no staff, and he didn't know how to do it. The Lord asked Brother Roberts if he had a shovel. Brother Roberts said that he did. Then the Lord told him to take the shovel, dig a hole, pray over it and break the ground for the university that he was going to build in Jesus' name.

Brother Roberts called some of his friends together and had a ceremony and did exactly as the Lord had told him. Brother Roberts had nothing but the word of the Lord and the image that God had given him. After that, money started pouring in from unexpected places to fund his university. As Brother Roberts prayed in the Spirit, whatever image God gave him of the layout of the campus or of how the buildings were to look, this is what he designed. This is how Oral Roberts University was built.

So imagine, picture, and dream about the visions God has given you. This is all a part of developing your faith. State what you are believing for, write it down, meditate on it, and picture it.

SEVEN STEPS TO INCREASE FAITH

Here are the seven steps to increase your faith that I always love to teach people. If you apply these to your life daily, you will definitely see your faith grow. Remember you already have faith. So employ it to agree with God's promises and stop agreeing with the devil's doubts.

1. God has given everyone a measure of faith (Rom. 12:3).

2. Exercise your muscle of positive faith daily through taking every thought captive to the obedience of Christ. Obey the Holy Spirit's leading and agree always with the Word of God.

3. "We walk by faith and not by sight" (2 Cor. 5:7). Don't look at the circumstances surrounding your life—they don't determine what happens. They are not set in stone. Circumstances can change in one moment through faith in God's promises and agreeing with them in prayer, and then trusting in Him. "The Word of the Lord is settled forever, it stands firm in heaven" (Ps. 119:89). "It will never return void, but it will accomplish all that God sends it to do" (Isa. 55:11).

4. Pray and ask God to reveal His promise for you and your life. Write down what you are specifically believing God for.

5. Thank the Lord that you have received what you have asked for, and so it will be done. Fix your mind and heart on God's promises. Meditate on what you are hoping for, visualize it— plant the seed in your mind (the thoughts of your heart) that you want to see grow and produce fruit. Declare it!

6. Hold the specific thing desired in your mind, think on it, and attach strong positive feeling toward seeing the fulfillment of God's promise. Have confidence that the things that God has promised to you and the things you are believing for will come to pass.

7. "Seek the kingdom of God first and His righteousness, and all these things shall be added unto you" (Matt. 6:25-34). And remember to be a giver—give of your time, talent, finances, your service, and of yourself. Jesus said, "If you give you will receive. Your gift will return to you in full measure, pressed down, shaken together to make room for more, and running over. Whatever measure you use in giving—large or small—it will be used to measure what is given back to you" (Luke 6:38 NLT).

chapter 14

THE DOMINION MANDATE

I have become too hot. I must cool myself and think; for it is
easier to shout, "Stop" than to do it.

—TREEBEARD
J. R. R. TOLKIEN, *THE LORD OF THE RINGS*

All authority has been given to Me in heaven and on earth.
Go, make disciples of all the nations, baptizing them ... Teach
them to do all that I have commanded you, and I will be with
you always, even to the end of the world.

—JESUS
MATTHEW 28:19-20

Jesus once asked His disciples, "Who do you say that I am?" Peter
answered and said, "You are the Christ, the Son of the living God."
Jesus replied, "Blessed are you Simon, son of Jonah, for this was
not revealed to you by man, but by My Father in heaven. And I tell
you...on this rock I will build my church, and the gates of Hell will
not overcome it" (Matt.16:15-18). The whole stream of history
since that time has been a fulfillment of Christ's prophecy.

THE ADVENT OF THE KINGDOM OF GOD

When Jesus began His ministry, He came preaching, saying, "The time has come, the kingdom of God is near. Repent and believe the good news!" (Mark 1:15). The advent of the coming "kingdom of God" had been foretold by Daniel almost 500 years earlier.

While the nation of Judah was being held captive in Babylon, King Nebuchadnezzar had a dream of a giant statue made of gold, silver, bronze, iron, and feet of iron mixed with clay. A stone cut out of the mountain suddenly struck the feet of the statue, causing it to come crashing down to the ground. The statue was crushed like chaff on the threshing floor and the wind blew it away, but the stone became a great mountain that filled the whole earth.

Many wise men in the Babylonian kingdom where called to tell the king what he had dreamed as well as the interpretation, but none could do this except the prophet Daniel because God revealed the king's dream and its interpretation to him. Daniel told the king that the statue represented various kings and their empires.

Then he foretold, "And in the days of those kings, the God of heaven will set up a kingdom which shall never be destroyed; no one will ever conquer it. It will shatter all these kingdoms into nothingness, but it will stand forever. That is the meaning of the rock cut from the mountain by supernatural means…the great God has made known to the king what will come to pass after this. The dream is certain, and its interpretation is sure" (Dan. 2:44-45 NLT).

In fulfillment of Daniel's prophecy, Jesus came preaching "the kingdom of God." He was "the God of heaven" who had come to "set up a kingdom that would never be destroyed." And where would that "kingdom" be established? Daniel decreed that it would start small, but would continue to grow until it would overthrow every kingdom of man and fill the entire earth.

Jesus referred again to His fulfillment of this passage from Daniel when He spoke to the Pharisees about their rejection of Him. "The stone which the builders rejected," Jesus said, "has become the chief cornerstone…Whoever falls on this stone will be broken: but on whomever it falls, it will grind him to powder" (Matt. 21:42, 44). Jesus identified with Daniel's prophecy and referred to Himself and His mission as the "stone" that would grind every other kingdom "to powder" and His kingdom as the one that would fill the earth and stand forever. In their resistance of Him, Jesus told the Pharisees, "The kingdom of heaven will be taken from you and will be given to a nation that will bear the fruits of it"(Matt. 21:43).

Isaiah also told about the extent of the dominion of Christ's kingdom in the following prophecy referring to Messiah's birth:

"Unto us a child is born, unto us a son is given, and the government shall rest upon His shoulders. And His name will be called Wonderful, Counselor, Mighty God, Everlasting Father, Prince of Peace. And *of the increase of His government and of His peace there will be no end*…to establish it with judgment and justice from that time forward, even forever. The zeal of the Lord of hosts will perform this" (Isa. 9:6-7).

Since the government of God fills Heaven in perfect peace, judgment and justice, where does His government, peace, judgment and justice need to increase? On earth! Jesus instructed His disciples to pray for this, saying, "Pray this way— Our Father in heaven, hallowed be Your name. *Your kingdom come, Your will be done on earth as it is in heaven*" (Matt.6: 9-10).

THE GREAT PROGRAM OF CHRISTIANITY

After Jesus began to preach, He went to Nazareth, entered the synagogue, opened a scroll, and read from the prophet Isaiah saying, "The Spirit of the Lord is upon Me, because He has anointed Me to preach the gospel to the poor; He has sent Me to heal the broken-hearted, to proclaim liberty to the captives and recovery of sight to the blind, to set at liberty those who are oppressed; to proclaim the favorable year of the Lord" (Luke 4:17-29 KJV).

Then Jesus said to all those in the synagogue who were staring at Him intently, "Today, this scripture is fulfilled in your hearing" (Luke 4:21). Jesus' mission encompassed more than just those who were alive in His day. He looked down the corridors of time and called for freedom from oppression and liberty for every captive who would look to Him at any age, in any century—He proclaimed Jubilee for the human race. He knew liberty and freedom must first begin in the human heart and would spread throughout this world as His kingdom was established in the hearts of mankind through the preaching of the Gospel and through the work of His sons and daughters.

The rest of this passage from Isaiah explains that those who are "redeemed" would "be called oaks of righteousness, the planting of the Lord that He may be glorified." His servants would be called "the priests of God." They would "rebuild the old ruins," and "raise up the former desolations, and repair the ruined cities, the desolations of many generations," so "God will cause righteousness and praise to spring forth before all nations" (Isa. 61:1, 4, 6,11).

Following this theme, Paul explains that the whole earth is waiting for "the revealing of sons of God…to be delivered from their bondage to corruption and into the glorious liberty of the children of God" (Rom. 8:21). And who are the sons of God? Paul tells us, "As many as are led by the Spirit of God, these are the sons of God" (Rom. 8:14). This is not gender specific, for Paul explains, "For you are all sons of God through faith in Christ Jesus. For as many of you as were baptized into Christ have put on Christ. There is neither slave nor free, there is neither male nor female; for you are all one in Christ Jesus" (Gal. 3:26-28).

All the liberty that has come to the human race since the beginning of the early church has been due to the work of God's sons—all those men and women who have been led by His Holy Spirit. This is the reason it is so imperative to the plans of God for each individual believer to learn to be led by the Holy Spirit.

THE CONQUERING POWER OF THE GOSPEL

Where was Christianity 2,000 years ago? Christianity consisted of a small group of men and women who had been commissioned by their resurrected Messiah to "make disciples of all nations" (Matt.28:19). The religious leaders of their own country persecuted them. They were opposed by the armed forces of the Roman Empire—the most powerful empire that had ever existed in the history of the world up to that time. Against such religious tradition and influence and military power, what chance did they have of survival?

Yet, Jerusalem was destroyed, Rome decayed from within, but the church stood strong, increased in number daily, and was victorious. The "gates of Hell" were not able "to prevail against" the church, because Something greater than a small band of dedicated people was there. That *Something* was and still is the Presence of the Resurrected Christ in the midst of His people.

Jesus promised His disciples, "Follow Me, and I will make you fishers of men" (Matt. 4:19). So Jesus showed His disciples that their success in "catching" people would depend on *following Him* and being led by His Holy Spirit. Again, when Jesus commissioned His disciples to take the Gospel to the nations, He didn't send them out in the strength of their own self-effort to hope for success, He promised, "And be sure of this: *I am with you always*, even to the end of the age" (Matt. 28:20 NLT). This fact is the power of the Gospel.

The most obvious thing that you can conclude from the progress of Christianity in history is that the Word of God not only has the power to conquer evil and overthrow oppression politically, it has actually done so. Men and women in all nations have been affected by the power of the Gospel.

Satan and the hordes of hell, religious leaders, Caesars, kings, tyrants, and dictators have fought against Jesus Christ and persecuted and killed His followers. Yet, down through the ages, one by one, those who have opposed Jesus and His kingdom, along with their failed philosophies, have been swept into the dustbin of history, while the kingdom of God and His church have come out of the struggle the clear winner.

The last 20 centuries have witnessed the progress of God's kingdom! The proclamation of the Gospel has overthrown monarchies, dictatorships, idolatry, slavery, communism, atheism, and human injustice of every kind. Christianity has not only survived for 2,000 years, it is still the fastest growing religion in the world because Christianity is, and always has been, culturally relevant.

HISTORY'S GREAT DIVIDE

Whether they realize it or not, every New Year the Western world celebrates Christ's victory. When Jesus Christ entered world history, His birth split history in two. In fact, all of time is defined by His advent—B.C. ("before Christ") and A.D.("Anno Domini," Latin for "in the year of our Lord"). The advent of Jesus Christ signified a new order for the human race. The Christian era is the only system in everyday use in the Western World to mark the passing of time, and the main system for commercial and scientific use in the rest of the world today. Even though some scholars have changed their definitions of this time period to B.C.E. (Before the Common Era) and C.E. (Common Era), our chronology of time still is based on the advent of Jesus Christ.

Paul foretells the progress of the Gospel: "This same Good News that came to you is going out all over the world. It is bearing fruit everywhere by changing lives, just as it changed your lives from the day you first heard and understood the truth about God's wonderful grace" (Col. 1:6, NLT).

MORE THAN A RESCUE MISSION

Muslims, in their effort to spread Islam today, say, "Take nations." Muslims have a worldview for total domination of the world. On the other hand many Christians only say, "Take converts," and focus on getting people to just "invite Jesus into their hearts." If we make the goal of our Christianity only a pietistic devotional life and a calendar full of attending church services, we have missed the point.

When Jesus rose from the dead and commissioned His disciples, He expounded on the work His disciples were to do. He had more in mind than having a group of followers who would spend most of their time in the four walls of a church building attending services just trying to make it to heaven when they die, or trying to get God to bless their family, their business, and their stuff so that they could have a peaceful life. His plan was not to have believers just focus on their devotional life, withdraw from the world, and retire to a monastery where they could focus on heavenly things. His commission was more extensive than just trying to save as many souls as possible off the "sinking ship" of earth.

Jesus gave a much broader mission to His disciples—He proclaimed, "All authority has been given to Me in Heaven and on Earth, so go and make disciples of all nations, baptizing them...Teach them to observe everything I have taught you"(Matt.

28:19-20). The disciples were to go everywhere preaching the good news of the "kingdom of God." This is the Christian worldview and has been called "the Great Commission."

Of course this is not a commission to force people to convert to Christianity by the edge of the sword or to force foreign kings and heads of state to submit to some ecclesiastical church or denomination—although the medieval church mistakenly tried this. Jesus made this clear when He told Pilate, "My kingdom is not of this world, if it were my servants would fight" (John 18:36). Then how do we bring the nations under His Lordship? We do this by winning hearts and minds to the Lord Jesus Christ—His kingdom is a spiritual kingdom to be established in the hearts of mankind.

Christ's Great Commission is a charge to His followers to instruct the citizens of nations to step down from the throne of their hearts in self-surrender and crown Jesus as King and Lord of all. It is a charge for people of every nation to end the "reign of self" and submit to His commandment of love. It is a commission to bring a "new creation" to birth, bearing the image and likeness of Jesus, and to teach people a new way to live—not by the impulses of the flesh, but through fellowship and friendship with God and in obedience to God's word and commands, to be empowered and led by His Holy Spirit.

It is God's desire for His kingdom to be established on earth "just as it is in heaven." Through a personal relationship with Jesus and the power of the indwelling Holy Spirit, Christians will be filled with God's love and His power. This will result in faith and spiritual direction that produce great deeds of righteousness. The stories in this book of Christians who have followed Jesus are testimonies to this fact. As we commit ourselves to obey Christ's commandments, His kingdom principles and His loving Presence manifested through the lives of His children will influence and change every area of society. The nations will be transformed.

chapter 15

A REVELATION OF JESUS CHRIST

There were ninety and nine that safely lay
In the shelter of the fold.
But one was out on the hills away,
Far off from the gates of gold.
Away on the mountains wild and bare.
Away from the tender Shepherd's care.

"Lord, you have here the ninety and nine;
Are they not enough for Thee?"
But the Shepherd made answer,
"There is one, who has wandered away from Me;
And although the road is rough and steep,
I go to the desert to find My sheep."

But none of the ransomed ever knew
How deep were the waters crossed;
Nor how dark was the night the Lord passed through
Until He found His sheep that was lost.
Out in the desert he heard its cry,
Sick and helpless and ready to die.

"Lord, what are those blood drops all the way
That mark out the mountain track?"
"They were shed for one who has gone astray

So the Shepherd could bring him back."
"Lord, why are your hands so rent and torn?"
"They are pierced tonight by many a thorn."
Then up through the mountains, thunder riven
And up from the rocky steep,
There arose a glad cry to the gate of Heaven,
"Rejoice, I have found my sheep!"
And the angels echoed around the throne,
"Rejoice, for the Lord brings back His own!"

THE NINETY AND NINE
BY ELIZABETH CLEPHANE
(1830-1869)

During the First Great Awakening in 18th century America, some people were discouraged by the large part of the world that was under the Islamic religion and wondered how these multitudes would ever be converted.

Jonathan Edwards encouraged them, "The visible kingdom of Satan shall be overthrown and the kingdom of Christ set up on the ruins of it, everywhere throughout the habitable globe…The kingdoms of Mahomet when God comes to appear will vanish away like a shadow and will disappear as the darkness in a room does when the light is brought in."[1] Here is the story of a young Moslem who is among the first-fruits of Edward's prophecy.

KAMRON'S STORY

My name is Kamron.[2] I was born in a Moslem nation to a loving family of mostly non-practicing Muslims. When I was 12, my father suffered near fatal injuries from an attempt on his life. Before his "accident" my father had acquired favor from the leader of our country to help local villagers by making a road that would allow them easier travel to and from the city. This road upset the wealthy landowners who in turn sent people out to run my father down with a car. Although he miraculously survived, he was never able to walk well again and continued to suffer physical setbacks. Consequently, I had to take over the family store at this very young age.

A few years later, at age 14, I received a dream. An angel appeared to me and gave me some Godly advice. In this visitation I could see God at a distance. In the religion of Islam it is unheard of for anyone other than the highest Muslim religious leaders to receive visions like this, so I wondered why I saw this. The vision stirred my spirit and caused me to think that there must be more to God than I had learned or knew. I believed that God must be calling me for a special purpose and decided to search for a God I could have a relationship with.

Through the Shiite Muslim religious practices, I became an avid seeker of Allah. To be a good Muslim it was important for me to pray five times a day in Arabic. Although I did not understand what I was praying, because my language was not Arabic, I was very earnest in my prayer. I read as many books on the Muslim religion as I could find, and spent many hours in conversations with religious leaders. I strove to have a relationship with God and desired a real connection with Him. I wanted to be God's friend but couldn't find my way to Him and felt so lost and out of place.

My pursuit of a true relationship with Allah left me angry and disappointed in a god with whom I couldn't have a relationship. Although I still had a deep longing in my heart to know God, I decided to give up my pursuit of Allah, since he didn't want to talk to me, and try to do something really big with my life.

When I was 29, I decided to leave Allah and my country behind and try to obtain a visa to go to the United States and make a fresh start. I did not tell anyone what I was about to do except my mother, who kept this a secret from the family. I knew it would upset my father terribly to have his oldest son leave. I was hoping my younger brother would step up and take my place in the family store. I had to get out.

A SUPERNATURAL ENCOUNTER

In a hotel, while waiting for my visa appointment, I obtained a Bible in my own language in the lobby of the hotel. I had never seen a Bible, much less one in my own language. To my surprise the hotel clerk said I could have it (Jesus was already at work!). In my hotel room I started to read this Bible. The names of Jesus would jump out of the pages, literally into the air, as I read. That night in a dream a Man appeared in front of me. I knew it was Jesus. He informed me He would get me into the United States, and He did.

The next day I went to the U.S. Embassy, stood in line, had a five-minute interview, and the lady handed me a visa. The people at the embassy were shocked. Very few people in my nation ever get a visa like this and, if they do, they have to wait for it for months or years, yet I went into the U.S. Embassy and got the visa that day. The person in line in front of me had a son in the United States, and he didn't get one.

When I returned to the embassy to pick up my visa the next day, a strange thing happened. As I approached the embassy someone walked out and handed the visa to me without me even going inside. As I left the embassy, I was careful to thank Allah for the visa because I thought this blessing came from him. Still I did not believe in Jesus at this time.

I got my stuff together, left for the U.S. and traveled to Atlanta to live with my aunt. Being frustrated with religion, as I knew it, I focused my attention on trying to become an actor and model in the United States. By another divine appointment, I ended up in an acting class led by a Spirit-filled Christian. My teacher took an interest in me, and one day she asked me to tell her about my religion and about my relationship with God. I told her that I had tried many years to get close to God and couldn't, and I was very disappointed and angry about it. She tried to talk to me about the love of God. This only stirred up my hurt and anger with religion. It made me angry for her to say that God was love.

Just imagine if you had tried to call someone for years and that person would never answer or call you back. You would certainly not think that person cared about you, much less loved you. Well, that's how I felt about God. I was angry because He never called me back or answered me when I tried to talk to Him. No, I could not accept that God was love. I also could not accept the idea that Jesus paid for my sin. I believed that each person must pay for his own sin. Every time my teacher talked to me about God, I felt very angry inside.

She ignored my response and kept reaching out to me. One day she invited me to a birthday party at her house. All the people there showed sincere interest in me. This really touched me. There, my teacher's roommate spoke to me about the love of God. I became very angry again and this time I started to cry and told her that I didn't want to talk about God any more. She kept talking to me anyway. I asked, "If God is a God of love, then why did He create Satan to deceive people?" I felt very angry and confused.

Suddenly a supernatural feeling came over me and I had a strong desire to pray and see if Jesus could help me find God. My teacher's roommate asked me if I would like to say the sinner's prayer with her to accept Jesus as my personal Savior. I said that I would like to say the prayer, but in my own way, and in my own language. My prayer was spontaneous and from my heart and this is what I said:

Jesus, I do not believe you are the Son of God, but if You are, I invite You to come into my heart. I do not believe Your blood has any power to forgive my sin, but if there is any forgiveness through Your blood, I accept it. If You can build a relationship between God, who created the whole world, and my heart, then, of course, I give You full permission to do anything You want with my life and my heart.

After praying my own salvation prayer to this new God, I turned to Allah and said, "Forgive me if I did anything wrong by praying this prayer. If Jesus is not your son, then stop Him from coming to me."

THE TIPPING POINT

After this my friends invited me to go to church with them and I said, "Yes." I went to church with them twice and felt so much peace. On my third visit, I was late to the service and was directed by the usher to go to the very front row and sit directly in front of the pastor. After about ten minutes, I could see the atmosphere change and a Man was standing behind the pastor who was preaching at that time. I asked myself, "Who is that," and a voice inside of me said, "Jesus." I mocked what I heard, and the Man (Jesus Christ) just walked inside of me. A fire came into my body and touched my heart so that I could not stop crying and shaking uncontrollably.

I was so embarrassed because I was crying in front of people without any reason while I was sitting in the very front row of a big church. After a couple of minutes I said, "Please don't do this to me, not now," meaning come back later. The moment I said this, the fire and crying stopped.

After the service, I told my friends what happened to me and they told me that I was touched by the Spirit of God. I was so amazed and excited at what they were telling me. The Holy Spirit of God was inside of me, with me, and I could know Him. They asked me, "Now do you believe that Jesus is the Son of God?" I said, "No, now I believe that Jesus lives and came to me. However, whether He is the Son of God is something He needs to convince me of personally."

Soon after this I went to another church with my friends. It was here I received targeted prophetic prayer, which brought intense deliverance. A group of people gathered around me and prayed for me and told me about my life and the supernatural encounter that I had with the angel in the dream when I was 14-years-old. I saw Jesus and was finally convinced that He was the Son of the Most High God.

This was the tipping point. My life was totally changed and I knew that it was not because of my efforts to be holy. Jesus had done it! I went up to the front of the church and I gave my life to Him. I remember looking around and it was as if I was seeing everything for the first time. Everything was new and beautiful, the people, even the carpet, the walls. For the first time I felt I was really alive.

Now I pursue Jesus everyday. My main goal is to be His best friend and to always draw closer and closer to Him until I am with Him in heaven. I have used my prayer of salvation to lead many other Muslims into His salvation and love. Many Moslems have all come to Jesus by praying this prayer that I now believe was given to me by the Holy Spirit in the day of my unbelief:

Jesus, I do not believe You are the Son of God, but if You are, I invite You to come into my heart. I do not believe Your blood has any power to forgive my sin, but if there is any forgiveness through Your blood, I accept it. If you can build a relationship between God, who created the whole world, and my heart, then, of course, I give You full permission to do anything You want with my life and my heart.

Those who have prayed this prayer with a sincere heart have all soon realized that their lives have been totally changed and they have done nothing to work at it. They have realized that Jesus transformed their lives and that He was the Son of God. The Holy Spirit has manifested Himself many times as they have repeated these words. They have had many visitations and visions of Jesus to help them in their journeys with Jesus, as many of them have no way to experience Christian fellowship.

I believe now that this salvation prayer came from God's heart for a people who need to know a God they can be close to and talk to—a God from whom they can receive love.

GOD'S CONTINUING BLESSING

My life's testimony is filled with many more miraculous interventions and messages, which I love to share, including my marriage to Suzy. My heart for the unsaved is to honestly introduce Jesus to all ages and people groups. I desire to help teach the church to share the Gospel in a very simple and powerful way.

I want to help the body of Christ enter into the true freedom that Jesus died for. I want to help "light" fresh fires in the hearts of Christians and rekindle old flames. I carry a burning passion in my heart for people to be turned on to a true love relationship with Jesus that goes deeper than the church has experienced so far. I finally found true love, and a relationship with the one true God, after so much searching and giving my life to a false god. Now I want to share my passion with the world.

I also have received simple guidelines from my prayer times with Jesus that are very helpful in daily Christian living. I love to impart these practical ways for us all to walk in more freedom and love through the power of the Holy Spirit. I would like to briefly share some of these thoughts with you.

HOPE, TRUST AND LOVE

Just imagine if the Lord had put His hope in Adam and Eve. That would have been a disaster. The more hope we place in people, the greater the disappointment. I have disappointed myself many times, and of course, other people have disappointed me. My disappointment in myself usually comes from me putting my hope in *my* strength, *my* gifting, and *my* ability to do things.

It is very important to let the Lord be our hope, and nothing else. We will face disappointment all of our lives unless we learn to put our hope in the Lord. Let us collect our scattered hopes from different places and give them all to Him. When we stop putting our hopes in other people or things, then the Lord can (and will) use other people, and those very things, to bless us. But first, He must be the source of hope, not any other.

This may sound so simple, but if we pay attention to it, it can set us free from anger, depression, hopelessness, confusion and unnecessary pain. Let us ask the Lord to forgive us for putting our hopes in other people, things and our own abilities. And let us not be angry with those who have disappointed us—we are guilty of doing the same thing.

Whatever you do, do it for the sake of love. If you don't, you'll end up wasting your life away. If we will use love for the foundation of what we do every day, then our lives will be simpler and filled with peace and joy. When love is not our foundation we can easily fall into depression, confusion, frustration and fear.

Seek love, follow love, desire love, learn to love, build with love, use love as a weapon, drink love, get fed by love, feed others with love, think through love, see through love, speak with love—love is the answer . . . love. Let us ask the Lord to help us to get to know love and to love.

LOOKING FOR JESUS

Every single day we have a choice to look for victory, or to look for Jesus. We can look forward to paying one more bill, receiving one more paycheck, facing one more giant and bringing it down, and getting many things accomplished, or we can look forward to seeing Him, the Son of the Most High, the Creator, each day.

Sometimes we welcome the chance to "get free" more than we welcome the opportunity to see Jesus. The apostle Paul and Silas focused more on seeing Jesus than getting out of prison. They began worshipping Jesus and they got out of prison supernaturally.

It's not about paying one more bill, receiving one more paycheck, getting out of debt, receiving one more healing, casting out one more demon. It's about Him FIRST. It's about seeing Him everyday. Life is full of challenges—we face one and overcome one, and another appears. It's not wise to spend our lives looking forward to solving our problems because problems are always there, they never stop coming at us.

When we stop looking forward to seeing victory and start looking forward to seeing Jesus, then we will see true victory (in all things) through Jesus in a supernatural way. Jesus has to be first. He wants us to see Him before we see victory. He wants our hearts to beat for Him first.

I don't want my heart to be in love with my dreams and desires. I don't want to send my heart after victory. I want my heart to be in love with Jesus Christ and always go after Him. Let us send our hearts after the precious Son of God. Let us look forward to seeing Him everyday.

SEVEN STEPS

I would like to end my testimony by asking you to consider following these seven steps to help you maintain a close relationship with God.

1. Give the Holy Spirit full permission and unlimited access to your heart and to your life. You had to invite Jesus into your heart once, but you need to give the Holy Spirit full permission and unlimited access over and over again.

2. Ask the Holy Spirit to go to the deepest parts of your heart and do as He wishes. Ask Him to help you to get connected to your own heart. Ask Him to teach you how to travel inside of your heart.

3. Choose to see the truth when He shows it to you. Choose to embrace His truths no matter how painful they are. He will happily help you.

4. Be extremely honest about your feelings with God and don't be afraid of telling Him the truth—He can handle it—He can even handle your anger and frustration toward Him. The more honest you get with the Lord, the closer friend you will become with Him.

5. Try to read God's word and spiritual messages with your heart, not your mind.

6. Pray that the Lord will give you the desire of your heart and that He will walk with you day and night.

7. Read through your heart, sing through your heart, and listen to the Holy Spirit, and what He shows you, through your heart. Your heart is not just for emotion. Your heart is much bigger than you think. Your heart is big enough for God Almighty to live in; your emotions are just a small part of your heart. Get your heart involved everyday. Have fun with the Holy Spirit.

chapter 16

A NEW MINDSET

Be diligent to show yourself approved to God...
rightly dividing the word of truth.

—PAUL

2 TIMOTHY 2:15

What you believe about the future will affect what you do today. You will never work for the transformation and redemption of society if you believe it's not possible. One of the biggest hindrances to Christians really believing in the conversion of the nations to the kingdom of God is what they believe about the future.

Many Christians hold a collapsing world-view. They have a dark picture of things getting worse and worse ending in Antichrist coming to take over the world. Consequently, they have no significant plans for the future. They feel that it is futile to polish brass on a sinking ship. Their goal is to save as many souls off this sinking ship of earth as possible, or more selfishly, their goal is to try to make themselves as comfortable as possible until they are suddenly whisked away to heaven in a secret rapture.

To understand where we are going and what the future holds, we must know where we have come from. This is why history is so important. The Jews refuse to accept the record of history about Jesus' death and resurrection. They reject Jesus' testimony about

His Divinity. They reject the testimony of the 500 witnesses who saw Him after His resurrection. As a result, they reject Jesus as the Messiah and look to the future for the fulfillment of prophecies concerning the Messiah that Jesus has already fulfilled.

Likewise, many things have happened over the past 2000 years of Church history. If we are ignorant of that history, or refuse to accept the testimony of history, we could make the same mistake as the Jews and look for the future fulfillment of scriptures that have already been fulfilled in ages past. This of course would give us a wrong perspective about the future.

A BRIEF HISTORY

According to the historical record, for over a period of 700 years of church history—between the 12th to the 19th centuries—there were a great number of spiritual Christians, revivalists, martyrs, and leaders of the Reformation who believed that the Apostasy (the falling away of the Church from the true faith) and the reign of the Man of Sin, or Antichrist, had found its fulfillment during the Medieval Ages.

This view was held by Christian leaders such as John Huss, Martin Luther, Sir Isaac Newton, George Fox, John Wycliffe, John Calvin, John Knox, William Tyndale, all the translators of the *King James Bible*, John Bunyan, Jonathan Edwards, John Wesley, the Founding Fathers of the United States of America, Charles Spurgeon, William Booth, and Charles Finney and many others.[1]

The translators of the King James Bible wrote a letter in the preface of the King James Bible in 1611 to King James which expresses the view of the Reformation concerning the fulfillment of Antichrist as having already taken place: "The zeal of Your Majesty toward the house of God…by writing in defense of the truth has delivered such a blow unto *that Man of Sin* as will not be healed."[2]

These leaders believed that scripture foretold that Antichrist was to arise from within the Church and had found its fulfillment in a particular succession of papal dynasties (2 Tim. 2:2-4). At that time in history, these papal leaders were not true shepherds of the flock of God. They primarily offered political and military leadership rather than the true spiritual life taught by Jesus. The Pope rode out at the head of his armies and used the sword to increase or defend his dominions.

During the Medieval Ages, the state and Church were joined together into the Holy Roman Empire. The kings of Europe swore allegiance to the Papal crown and pledged their swords to fight to defend it and to uphold the doctrines of the Church. If they failed to do so, according to Church doctrine, they would be excommunicated from the Church and their souls would be condemned to the fires of hell. England was punished this way a number of times, their churches were closed, people were refused the mass which left them at the precipice of hell until the king complied to the Pope's wishes.

These leaders also believed that the Apostasy of the Church resulted from the Church being controlled by the state for a period of 1500 years during what we now call the Medieval or Dark Ages and that they were seeing the results of it in their day. Church offices were bought and sold for political power and prestige and were not given as a result of someone's spiritual depth, holiness of life, or spiritual maturity.

Pardon for sin could be bought for money. Money could be given to help release people from Purgatory so they could go to heaven. As a result, corruption within the Church was widespread. While there were still some very spiritual people among its ranks, many of its leaders were full of self-interest, rather than sacrificial love.

The Bible was a forbidden book. Church authorities often made decrees to put people who read the Bible to death if they were not priests—and yet very few of the priests had actually studied it. As a result, preaching consisted of strange tales and the wisdom of men, and consequently, many errors came into the Church. When Wycliffe and others began to translate the Bible into the language of the people and make it accessible to the common man, they were persecuted and hunted like common criminals and some were executed by the religious authorities.

Instead of the world persecuting Christians, Church leaders persecuted those who did not agree with them, killing those who refused to join or believe in their teachings. This practice resulted in the travesties that took place during the Crusades and the Inquisition. As a result of the fear of persecution or death, masses of unconverted people flocked into the Church and brought their heathen practices into it, being forced to join or face the sword.

THE REFORMATION

During the 16th century, Martin Luther, a Catholic priest and Biblical scholar, made an attempt to reform the Roman Church from within and bring it back to the truths taught in the Holy Scriptures. From many years of studying the Bible, Luther believed that the Bible taught that people were not saved by works—buying pardons for sins, paying to get the dead out of purgatory, making special pilgrimages to holy places, giving money to build churches, doing penance (self-punishment or an act of religious devotion performed to show sorrow for having committed a sin), worshiping relics, saying matins (special morning prayers) etc.

He taught that people were saved through faith in the shed blood of Jesus Christ for the forgiveness of sins. At the time, the Roman Church did not accept Luther's work and forced him out of the

Church. The Pope sent out a decree that excommunicated Luther and condemned him to the fires of hell.

Hundreds of thousands of people joined Luther in his exile, finding new freedom in Christ. This began a period of history known as the Protestant Reformation. Europe burst into flames as some of the kings of Europe and the religious authorities tried to force the Protestants back into the Roman Church.

In France alone, 70,000 Protestants were slain in a few days, and over a period of 30 years, 760,000 people were killed. In Ireland, persecution of Protestants resulted in more than 200,000 Protestants being killed in a few days—the idea was to rise up and kill all the Protestants at once.[3] This is the root of the great feuds between Catholics and Protestants that have continued in Ireland into the late 20th century. More Christians were killed during this time than all the early Christians martyred by the Caesars combined.

Many of those who wanted to reform the Roman Church found themselves outside it. A number of European nations decided that now was the time to break away from the Roman Church. These nations established Reformed Churches in an attempt to correct what they believed to be the errors of Rome. The Reformed Churches were controlled by the state and continued some of the barbaric practices in the spirit of Antichrist. In England, when the Catholics were in power they killed the Protestants, when the Protestants were in power they killed the Catholics.

Struggles went on all over Europe as the battle raged against "the spirit of Antichrist" for freedom of thought, the right to worship God according to the dictates of conscience, and the right of the common man to read and understand the Bible for himself without any intermediary. Switzerland broke away from the Roman Catholic Church, and leaders of the Reformation established the Reformed Church there. However, the Church and state were still joined together.

Eventually those in Switzerland who did not believe exactly as the Reformed Church believed were persecuted. People were thrown into prison for refusing to attend the Swiss Church because they wanted to worship with the group they felt had the true doctrine. This group was called by their enemies Anabaptists. They rejected the idea of infant baptism and believed only those who were true believers could be baptized—because how can a baby repent of sins?

Furthermore they believed that baptism by immersion and not sprinkling was the true way to baptize. The Anabaptists lost their property, were imprisoned, exiled, or killed. Those who survived this persecution fled to Holland and then to the New World and are now known as the Mennonites and Amish.

England made its final separation from Rome and established the Church of England, also called the Anglican Church. The Bible was taken out of the Latin and published in English and made available to the people. From studying the word of God, it was evident to many thoughtful Christians that reform was still needed in the churches of the Reformation.

As a result, a group of believers called the Puritans worked to reform the Church of England. However, England's state church, was still infected with the spirit of Antichrist and fueled by the fires of "pride and selfish ambition."[4] The state church persecuted the Puritans for their beliefs, imprisoned some, and others fled to Holland in exile. John Bunyan, a well-known Puritan, wrote *Pilgrim's Progress* from prison in England having been jailed for his Puritan beliefs that were different from the Anglican Church.

THE FOUNDATIONS OF THE NEW WORLD

Finally, Christians who were persecuted in England and Europe came to America seeking religious freedom. One of these groups was the Pilgrims who had fled to Holland in exile to escape persecution in England. They were *not* seeking to reform the Anglican

Church, but instead wanted to return to the practices of primitive Christianity. They looked forward to the day foretold in Scripture when they believed the nations would one day turn to the Gospel of Jesus Christ. Because of this hope, by faith they left civilized Europe and crossed treacherous waters to journey to the wilderness of North America to found a new beachhead for Christianity.

It was their belief that the reign of Antichrist and the Apostasy of the Church (which had lasted for 1,200 years) was coming to a close. This faith gave the Founders of North America the courage to start the world over again in what they called the "New World." In the New World they looked for a greater reformation and transformation of Christianity. Here they began to carve out a new nation where religious liberty would be the heritage of all.

William Bradford writes in *History of Plymouth Plantation* that the Pilgrims had "a great hope and inward zeal of laying some good foundation for the propagating and advancing the Gospel of the kingdom of Christ" even through they might be "steppingstones" for the great work to follow.[5] It was the Pilgrims' hope to see the Church reformed and returned to its "ancient purity" and recover its "primitive order, liberty and beauty."[6]

Many of the Puritans also left England and came to what is now Boston. The Puritans were different from the Pilgrims in that they were trying to reform the Anglican Church. At first, the Puritans in the New World were still affected by the spirit of Antichrist. They used civil authorities to persecute members of the community who didn't believe exactly as they believed. Roger Williams, Ann Hutchinson, and other members of the community were forced into exile. For some of them, this meant certain death among the Indians. Others were not allowed to vote or were put to death for refusing to conform. Mary Dyer was hung for refusing to renounce her faith as a Quaker.

Finally, most people came to see the necessity of religious freedom. The framers of the United States Constitution wanted to protect the individual Christian believers from persecution from the state. Practically all the delegates that worked to draw up the Constitution were Christians and some were ministers.

The Founding Fathers believed religious freedom was so important that they enshrined it into law as the first article in the Bill of Rights to guarantee the right of every citizen to believe and worship God as they wished without fear of being persecuted by the government. Article One states: "Congress shall make no law respecting an establishment of religion, or prohibiting the free exercise thereof…" The Founders' goal was not to protect the government from Christianity, or to protect the citizens of the country from religion; their goal was to protect Christians from persecution *by the government.*

By studying the original documents and letters of the Founders of our nation, it is obvious that the majority of them looked toward a future in which the nations would be converted to Christ, when according to the prophets, "all the world" would know Christ's righteousness, and "would worship Him and sing praises to His name" (Ps. 66:4). They looked for the golden age promised by the prophets when all the nations would serve the Lord Jesus Christ.

The Founders of the New World in North America looked for the advancement of the kingdom of God on earth, and a return to the simplicity of the early Church. They believed that Peter, under the anointing of the Holy Spirit, referred to the necessity of the fulfillment of all Biblical prophecy before Jesus would return when Peter emphasized that Jesus must "remain in heaven until *the restoration of all things spoken by the mouth of God's holy prophets since time began"*(Acts 3:21).

PROPHECIES OF CHRIST'S VICTORY IN THE NATIONS

And what are some of the prophecies that have not yet been fulfilled? David declared, "All the ends of the world shall remember and turn to the Lord: all the families of the nations shall worship before You. For the kingdom is the Lord's and He rules over the nations" (Ps. 22:27-28). And of the universal triumph of Christ's kingdom the Psalmist declared, "Arise, O God, judge the earth: for You shall inherit all nations" (Ps. 82:8). "All nations that You have made shall come and worship before You, O Lord; and shall glorify Your name" (Ps. 86:9). And Isaiah prophesied:

> And it shall come to pass in the last days, that the mountain of the Lord's house shall be established in the top of the mountains, and shall be exalted above the hills; and all nations shall flow unto it. And many people shall go and say, "Come let us go up to the mountain of the Lord, to the house of the God of Jacob; and He will teach us his ways, and we will walk in His paths;" for out of Zion shall go forth the law, and the word of the Law from Jerusalem.
>
> And He shall judge among the nations, and shall rebuke many people; and they shall beat their swords into plowshares, and their spears into pruning hooks; nations shall not lift sword against nation, neither shall they learn war any more" (Isa. 2:2-4).

Where did Isaiah say that war would be no more? This must very obviously take place on earth because there are no weapons in heaven to be turned to plowshares. *When* did Isaiah say this would take place? In the *last days*. Peter explains that the outpouring of the Holy Spirit on the day of Pentecost was the signal that the *last days* had begun: "And it shall come to pass in the *last days*," says God, "that I will pour out of My Spirit on all flesh" (Acts 2:17). Peter identified the "last days" as the age of Christianity.

The foundations of the United States of America were laid in the faith of the Protestant Reformation. In 1874, Charles Spurgeon, British minister and one of the most highly influential among the Reformed Christians, summed up Reformation faith in his book, *The Treasury of David*, commenting on Psalm 86:9:

> David was not a believer in the theory that the world will grow worse and worse, and that the dispensation will wind up with general darkness, and idolatry. Earth's sun is to go down amid tenfold night if some of our prophetic brethren are to be believed.
>
> Not so do we expect, but we look for a day when the dwellers in all lands shall learn righteousness, shall trust in the Savior, shall worship Thee alone O God 'and shall glorify Thy name.' The modern notion has greatly damped the zeal of the Church for missions and the sooner it is shown to be unscriptural the better for the cause of God. It neither consorts with prophecy, honors God, nor inspires the church with ardor.[7]

THE BELIEVER'S PROMISE OF INHERITANCE

Before there was a Church or even the Ten Commandments written on tablets of stone, Abraham walked with God. The New Covenant points out Abraham's faith as an example for every true believer. Abraham walked with God, and wherever he went, he built an altar to the Lord. Paul reminds us that God's promise that true believers would "inherit the world" was given to all those who walk in the faith of Abraham through Christ. "The promise that he would be the *heir of the world* was not to Abraham or to his seed through the law, but through the righteousness of faith" (Rom. 4:13).

God promised that through Abraham and his Seed (Christ) all the earth would be blessed. "And now that you belong to Christ, you are the true children of Abraham. You are his heirs, and God's promise to Abraham belongs to you" (Gal. 3:29 NLT). Jesus promises this inheritance of the world in His Sermon on the Mount saying, "Blessed are the meek for they shall inherit the earth" (Matt. 5:5).

BEING A FAITHFUL STEWARD OF YOUR TALENTS

Paul gives us a dramatic picture of Jesus' return saying, "The Lord Himself will descend from heaven with a shout with the voice of the Archangel and the trump of God and the dead in Christ shall rise first"(1 Thes. 4:16). Until that day, Jesus clearly taught His disciples that they should always use all their gifts and abilities for His glory to increase His kingdom until He returns.

In the parable of the distribution of the talents, Jesus makes this clear. Although the word "talents" in the King James Version of the Bible represents a sum of money, because of the wide distribution of this Bible in the English speaking world, the word "talent" came to mean in the English language "the gifts and abilities that God has given to you"[8]

In this parable Jesus explained, "The kingdom of heaven (or of God) is like a man traveling to a far country, who called his own servants and delivered his goods to them. And to one he gave five talents, to another two, and to another one, to each according to his own ability; and immediately he went on a journey." (Jesus used "the kingdom of heaven" and "the kingdom of God" interchangeably as meaning the same thing.)

Both the man who had been given the five talents, and the man who had been given two talents used the talents that they had been given and invested them and multiplied them. But the man who had received one talent, hid the talent he had "because he was afraid."

Jesus explained that when their master returned, he asked his servants to give an account of their stewardship over the things he had given them. To the men who had used and multiplied their talents he said, "Well done, good and faithful servant; you have been faithful over a few things, I will make you ruler over many things. Enter into the joy of your lord."

But to the man who had hidden his talent because he was afraid, his master said, "You wicked and lazy servant…so you ought to have deposited my money with the bankers, and at my coming I would have received back my own with interest. So take the talent from him, and give it to him who has ten talents…and cast the unprofitable servant into the outer darkness. There will be weeping and gnashing of teeth'" (Matt. 25:14-30).

In this parable, Jesus points out that the blessing of using our talents would be leadership and increased responsibility—"faithful over a few things, ruler over many things." He reminds us that the sin of not using our talents until He returns would result in the loss of everything, even the loss of our lives to uttermost darkness. From this parable it is evident that Jesus is not seeking to give us less responsibility. He wants to give us more responsibility when we are faithful to use what He has already given us.

BRINGING THE LOST WORLD INTO CHRIST'S KINGDOM

When Jesus called His disciples, He said to them, "Follow Me, and I will make you fishers of men" (Matt. 4-18-20). Jesus has given us the great privilege to reach the lost for Him. There is no greater blessing than to see someone who is lost become a follower of Jesus Christ. The good news is that we don't have to try to save the lost in our own strength and effort, but as we follow Jesus, He will do it through us.

While this was Jesus' primary assignment for His disciples, the focus on winning the world to Jesus has been lost by a great number of Christians in America. They have exchanged a Christ-centered Gospel for a focus that is self-centered—"God bless my wife, my husband, my children, my life, my business, my career, and my stuff. Give me prosperity, peace, and happiness. Amen." Church growth in the United States has been like a game of musical chairs as people go from church to church continually looking for greener pastures. Keith Greene illustrated this problem in an analysis of a poll that was taken in 1933. The poll stated that there were 7,000 churches in America that didn't win one soul to Jesus that whole year! Keith reasoned, "If preachers preached only an average of 42 weeks, two times every Sunday, not including any extra meetings or midday meetings, that would mean that these 7,000 ministers preached approximately 560,000 sermons in one year. Think about the lights for their church building, the salaries, and all their expenses for this one-year to make this possible. Yet, 560,000 sermons preached by 7,000 ministers to approximately 12 million hearers during a process of 12 months failed to bring a single soul to Christ that year."

Keith reasoned, "There is something radically wrong with this. Either there was something radically wrong with these 7,000 ministers, or their 560,000 sermons, or with both." Keith then contrasted the emphasis for ministers laid out by John Wesley during the Great Awakening in the 18th century who looked at soul winning as their ONLY task.

John Wesley, founder of Methodism who in their day were radical soulwinners, summarized the goal for his ministers: "You have nothing to do, but save souls, therefore spend and be spent in this work, it is not your business to preach as many sermons as possible, but to bring as many sinners to repentance and save as many souls as you possibly can, and to build them up in that holiness without which they cannot see the Lord."[9]

Consider the results of John Wesley's emphasis on soul winning in the 18th century. During the spiritual awakening that was taking place in England, John Wesley made an urgent appeal to the

Methodist societies to send missionaries to America to perpetuate the work that God had begun in England in the American colonies. Francis Asbury was the man who answered that call to take the message of the new birth/the new nature, the love of God, and holiness of heart and life to the frontiers of America. Asbury left behind his mother and father, never to see them or his homeland again, and set his face toward America. In 1771, when Asbury arrived in Philadelphia at the age of 26 he was Wesley's youngest foreign missionary.

Upon Asbury's arrival in North America, one in 5,000 colonists were Methodists. So great was the sweeping effects of revival and the preaching of his circuit riders, who took the Gospel on horseback across the colonies and American frontier, that when Asbury died 45 years later, one in every 40 Americans were Methodists.[10] In that day, the Methodists were the greatest soul-winning society in America. Over 28 denominations other than the Methodist Church sprung from Wesley's roots including the modern-day Pentecostal, Charismatic, and Faith movements.

Those who were affected by the Wesleyan revival of total surrender to the Lordship of Jesus Christ and the new birth experience, not only won souls, they went on to disciple the nations. The Methodists in the United States eventually established hundreds of hospitals as well as over 1200 colleges and universities; they spawned asylum reform, the abolition of slavery, the Women's Movement, and the Temperance Movement. Sunday schools, as well as relief agencies for the poor, unheard of in history before Methodism, sprang up everywhere. In 1915, Woodrow Wilson, 28th President of the United States, delivered an address at Wesleyan University on the occasion of the Wesley Bicentennial. President Wilson reflected on John Wesley's place in history:

> Everything that made for the regeneration of the times seemed
> to link itself with Methodism. The great impulse of humane feeling

which marked the closing years of the century seemed in no small measure to spring from it: the reform of prisons, the agitation for the abolition of slavery, the establishment of missionary societies and Bible societies, the introduction into life, and even into law, of pity for the poor, and compassion for those who must suffer. The noble philanthropies and reforms, which brighten the annals of the nineteenth century, had their spiritual birth in the eighteenth. Wesley had carried Christianity to the masses of the people, had renewed the mission of Christ himself, and all things began to take color from what he had done…

There is a deep fascination in this mystery of what one man may do to change the face of his age. John Wesley, we have had reason to say, planned no reform, premeditated no revivification of society; his was simply the work of an efficient conviction…What is important for us is the method and the cause of John Wesley's success. His method was as simple as the object he had in mind. He wanted to get at men, and he went directly to them, not so much as a priest, but rather as a fellow man standing in a like need with themselves. And the cause of his success? …

A clear conviction of revealed truth and of its power to save…The eighteenth century cried out for deliverance and light, and God had prepared this man to show again the might and the blessing of His salvation.[11]

To Disciple Nations

Recognizing the need today for Christians to disciple nations, Bill Bright, founder of Campus Crusade for Christ, and Loren Cunningham, founder of Youth With A Mission, met together one day and both presented an exact vision that they had each received from the Lord. This vision entailed seven mountains of influence that Christians must invade with the principles of Christ's kingdom in order to lead and influence a nation and win the world for Jesus

Christ. They explained that whoever controls these mountains of power will have influence over all of society. Whoever can take these areas will take nations. The seven mountains were as follows: Church, Family, Education, Media, Performing Arts (including Entertainment and Sports), Commerce (including Science and Technology), and Government (including Politics).

Jesus said, "The Gospel of the kingdom will be preached to all nations and then the end will come" (Matt. 24:14). The Gospel of the kingdom is about a government—Christ's government, which begins in the hearts of men, women, and children and will flow out of redeemed men and women to be reflected in national life. It is about the laws of nations that they may be just, humane and compassionate, so that all nations might have the opportunity to enjoy prosperity, blessing, freedom, and liberty to serve God according to their own heart and conscience. The Gospel of the kingdom is about a new world order—the order of the kingdom of God.

Unfortunately because so many Christians today live only in the bubble of church life, Christians have lost their influence in many arenas of society. They have abdicated their responsibility and have not provided leadership or realized the importance of having the spiritual maturity and an adequate education so they can lead society. Jesus told His disciples, "You are the salt of the earth. If the salt has lost its flavor, it is good for nothing but to be thrown out and trampled under foot by man"(Matt. 5:13).

Many Christians today get upset about how our schools, the media and the government are changing their culture for the worse. When you get mad, ask yourself: why aren't you there? Why aren't you the one influencing that arena? Why are people with poor character and morals dictating what we, as a nation and world, have to see and be a part of? Why are those who teach anti-Christian materials and things that are an abomination to God teaching the children in this nation's schools? Why are the majority of the professors at the universities against conservative Christian values and determined to try to destroy a young person's faith in Christ?

BECOMING SALT AND LIGHT

The truth is that if the Christians do not provide the ideas and leadership that govern society, someone else will. Someone will lead, some philosophy will dominate—the question is which one? If we don't take charge and work to change the world through our obedience to the Holy Spirit and the call God puts on our life, then those who want to keep abortion legal and want to remove God and His laws from our constitution, pledges, educational, and legal systems, will take charge and lead the way.

Understand the area that God has called you to influence and be salt and light. This will help you direct and focus the energy of your life toward specific goals rather than wasting your time doing odds and ends of things that have nothing to do with your central focus. Ask God for open doors and for specific direction for your life's work that will best help in establishing His kingdom. Find out God's will and do it! Pour the energies of your life into it! Look for God to direct you into that which is impossible in your own strength, but possible with faith in God.

Doing your best at school and putting forth your best effort in your job is representing Jesus with excellence. The scriptures tell us that a person "who is diligent in his work" will bear rule, have riches, and "stand before kings" (Prov. 10:4,12:24,22:29). If you are not good at school or work, ask Jesus to teach you the things you don't know, He will! There is no absence of intelligence in His Presence. I have never heard of someone getting worse grades when they get saved—they usually get better ones.

Whatever vision Jesus has put in your heart, start training for it at an early age. And if you are older, it is not too late. Ask God for vision and direction, and with that vision, ask God for a plan. "A man plans his ways, but the Lord orders His steps" (Prov. 16:9).

Some have taken this scripture to mean that it is bad to plan your ways and that the Lord is going to do everything. Consequently they make plans for nothing and just live "hand to mouth." For example, if you feel called to be a doctor, you obviously will have to go to medical school. The Lord can change your plans as you move along, but He can't even adjust you when you're not moving. Light is given for the path ahead each time we take a step of faith.

We are called to bring Christ's kingdom in every sphere of influence in our society, nation, and world through Christian love and service. If you will "listen to the commands of the Lord and carefully obey them, the Lord will make you the head and not the tail, above and not beneath," and we will see this world and our generation changed for Jesus Christ (Deut. 28:13).

chapter 17

DISCIPLE THE NATIONS

How then shall they call on Him in whom they have not
believed? And how shall they believe in Him of whom they
have not heard? And how shall they hear without a preacher?
And how shall they preach unless they are sent?

—PAUL
ROMANS 10:14

This is a story about a Chinese man who began to seek for the
meaning of life as a child. Because of religious persecution in
China, I will call his name Chien to protect his identity. Chien was
touched through an American English teacher at his university in
China and now is on fire to change the world for Jesus Christ.

CHIIEN'S STORY

I was ten-years-old when I began to think about what would
happen to me when I died. I had no answers and was only filled
with fear and confusion.

When I was 14, I joined a Chinese spiritual cult. It was very
evil, and I was involved in this cult for seven years. Through this, I
tried to pursue spiritual power and tried to find out what the
meaning of life was, and where I would spend eternity, but I never
found these answers. During these years, I influenced many young
people to join this cult and tried to place all my energy in it. Eight

years later, I still had found no hope and no answers from this cult; all I felt was frustration. I was twenty-two-years-old.

When I was 25, I had an American teacher at my university. I later found out that he was a Christian, and I kept asking him questions about the spiritual world. One night, he told me about Jesus and I decided to accept Jesus' love and sacrifice for me and become a Christian.

After I became a Christian, my life and spirit changed dramatically. Whenever, I prayed to Jesus, He answered me with great power and blessings. The American teacher, his wife, and friends prayed for me especially and drove a lot of demons out of me. I was set free. The greatest peace had come into me by the Holy Spirit.

New Beginnings

I began to evangelize all the people around me—my own family, my friends, classmates, and my professors. Many of them accepted the Gospel with great joy. They received joy in their hearts and minds that they had never experienced before. I began to establish great friendships among the new believers, who were mostly intellectuals. At this point in my life, I didn't know I was called into the ministry.

As time went on, I gradually had more and more influence among the churches in China, and I finally understood the plan that God had for me. At the age of 30, I began to minister to the Muslims in China. I wrote a few books for the kingdom of God that had great impact among the Chinese people, and I am astonished at how the Lord Jesus could use me in such a powerful way.

After this, I felt the Lord leading me to come to the United States to preach the Good News among the Chinese intellectuals on the university campus. This is a new ministry for me, and there have been a lot of surprises along the way. Over the years, the Lord continually gave me the vision that we can change China for Him by influencing the intellectuals studying in America. Now he is using me to do it! These students will go back to China and become the next politicians, businessmen, doctors, lawyers, and leaders of my nation!

I am amazed and so grateful, whenever I think about my past life before I met Jesus. It has been only ten years since I was saved, and only God could take me from dust to be a totally new creature, a noble child of His. And the most important thing is that I have the answer to the questions I began thinking about when I was ten. I get to spend eternal life with Jesus and live my life now with rich, true meaning for Him

જી જ જી

God is using Chein to bring Christianity to China's future leaders. In 1949, there were 700,000 Protestants when the Communists took over China. Open doors spokesman said they estimate between 60 to 80 million Christians in China today in the underground churches.

chapter 18

TO BRING HIS KINGDOM

He lifts the beggar from the ash heap and
makes him inherit the throne of glory.

—1 SAMUEL 2:8

Our final story is from a former prostitute in the Ukraine who became a Christian and learned that God had called her to take dominion over evil and to bring His kingdom on earth as it is in heaven. God took this empty and lonely person, filled her with His love, and is using her to change the Ukraine!

TATYANA GALUSHKO'S STORY

My name is Tatyana and I was born into a family where my mother and father were both alcoholics. My father left my mother when I was young. I didn't receive love at home, so I was very violent at school and no one understood me. My life seemed empty and I had nothing to live for, so I experimented with everything the world had to offer. I had a child by the time I was 17-years-old.

As a result of being addicted to drugs and alcohol for 11 years, I was having a hard time making enough money for my baby and myself. I was introduced to the lifestyle of prostitution, which was part of my life for four years. I was so empty that I had nothing to give to my daughter. My whole life I had always wanted be the best mom and love my daughter, but instead I was putting her through so much. Because of my lifestyle, my daughter had to stay with my mother.

A few clients that I had from prostitution tried to murder me, and many times death was just breathing down my neck. One time a guy hung me from eight stories high trying to kill me, someone once tried to drown me, and I experienced many other attempts on my life. Then one day I went to Pastor Sunday's church in the Ukraine. There I met Jesus and He changed my life! I went through months of deliverance and Jesus set me free!

LIVING A LIFE OF PURPOSE

The experiences I had in school led me to want to help those young people in the same position I was once in. My hardest times had been during my school days when all I wanted was to just be loved, understood, and accepted. The lack of this led me to failure in my behavior and academics.

After I was saved, my pastor, Sunday Adelaja, encouraged me to do some type of ministry for young people. One day Bill Wilson, based in New York City, came to speak to us about his ministry to many children all around the world. When I heard him speak, it really touched my heart. I felt the Lord leading me to go and get further education so that I would be in a better position to help children. In May 2002, Bob Weiner came to my church in Ukraine. As he spoke I couldn't sit in one place because the fire that he came with just hit me. I wanted to do something to help extend God's kingdom on earth, and God gave me a plan.

I had a real burden for the young people of the Ukraine. Generally, most of the children in the Ukraine are ignored by their parents. No one really cares if they do well in school, what they do with their life, or what happens to them. The children and teenagers have no real friends that are adults who can offer them personal advice and counseling. For example, one young girl of 14 asked her friend what she should do because she had no adults to advise her. Her boyfriend wanted to have sex with her, or he was going to break up with her. Her friend told her to go ahead and have sex with him because he was such a cool guy. Well, that cool guy broke up with that young girl when she was 8 months pregnant.

The indifference of their parents leads children to the inevitable consequences of pain and disappointment—early pregnancy, prostitution, and venereal diseases. The teenagers also have low self-esteem and no vision for their lives. I know that the children are the ones who will change the Ukrainian nation so that it will have a bright future, and when they are saved the revival of the Ukrainian nation will begin.

DIVINE STRATEGY

The Lord led me to develop a plan to reach out to the Ukrainian school children. I visit the schools, along with those who are helping me, and we all try to encourage the children by showing them respect, by caring about their ideas, and by trying to give them vision and purpose. We teach them what true friendship is about and teach them that real beauty comes from the inner person. Many of these students do not understand the reason that they are studying, so we explain the importance of knowledge.

We also include such topics as protection from psychological and physical violence, the difference between love and lust, the roots of AIDS and HIV, the danger of drugs, tobacco and alcohol, and the importance of obedience to their parents and respect for aged people. We teach the male students the importance of a man's virginity, manhood, responsibility, honor, and the importance of being successful.

If Christians don't visit the schools and tell children about Jesus and teach them Christian values, then someone else will visit the schools and offer them drugs and alcohol and lead them into occult practices. As Christians, Jesus has given us a commandment to take dominion over our culture and nations. He gives us His power to fulfill this task. I asked Him: "Lord, if we are all made to dominate, whom will we rule?" God showed me that He has created people so that they dominate over everything, but not over each other. When a person builds his life on God's plan there will be no place for domination over people, we are called to serve. Jesus said, "All authority has been given to Me in heaven and on earth. Go therefore and make disciples of all the nations... teaching them to observe all things that I have commanded you; and lo, I am with you always, even to the end of the age" (Matt. 28:18-20). We are in the process of doing just that.

Transforming a Nation

My ministry is now three-years-old, and we are reaching out daily to 18,000 teenagers throughout Kiev, as well as reaching out to 6,000 teenagers in the 19 surrounding areas. We also have student ministries in twenty other cities in the Ukraine, and two in Russia and in Moldova. So right now we are working with about 60,000 teenagers.

The government is supporting our work to help teach the teenagers Christian values and principles for successful living. The government pays for our expenses, whether it is an auditorium or anything else we might need. The government also pays for my salary and the salaries of the people that work with me.

There is, of course, a chain of command in the government of the school system; one person cannot have full control over the schools in so many cities. Consequently, the government asked me to recruit people from the church to put in the chain of command over the education system in the cities. The government then puts the God-fearing people from church in those positions of leadership in the school system as they become available.

Recently, I was talking to God and I told Him, "I am going to change the whole education system." Soon, I received a phone call from the lady in charge of the education system in the Ukraine. She said that she liked the program I had written for the teenagers and felt that it was very professionally written. Then she asked me if I could help her change Ukraine's education system. This is just what I believed was going to happen.

I am going to be making a lot of drastic changes in what the students in the Ukraine are being taught in their textbooks from grades 1 to 12. Although I am the main person working on the textbooks, there are many others who are helping from the church. The main thing I talk about and change in these textbooks is moral ethics; other people are working on other subjects. When the lady in charge of the education system read the book that I had written about my life and my testimony, she was in total shock because of the way that God has changed my life.

As I was talking to her, she told me that she herself could not fire all the people who had been writing the textbooks for the schools, even though she understands that it is not truth—for example, the subject of evolution. However, she also believed that God Himself wanted to take these people out of their positions so that the nation of Ukraine could be changed toward truth. Thankfully, the Ukraine hasn't gone as far as the United States and has not become so scary as to permit crazy social changes such as same sex marriage. We know that with this change toward Christianity in our educational system, society will also make a big change and the Ukraine will become a godly nation.

We are also working with the local state bodies on youth and family policy in Kiev and the Kiev region. We are starting a project that will cover 12 cities and regions of the Ukraine. In addition our school ministry now works in 20 cities in the Commonwealth of Independent States, an association of former Soviet republics that was established in December 1991 by Russia, Ukraine, and Belarus. Other members include Armenia, Azerbaijan, Georgia, Kazakhstan, Kyrgyzstan, Moldova, Tajikistan, Turkmenistan, and Uzbekistan.

Articles devoted to the problems of pupils are regularly published in the newspapers of the state body on youth and family policy. We also give advice to teachers who don't know how to solve the problems of drug addiction, alcoholism and prostitution. The Lord also directed us to work with pupils when they were out of class. We are opening image clubs for girls where they will be taught how to care for their appearance and how to have proper hygiene.

We asked students to give their ideas for the youth centers we are starting. These are the student's ideas which we will be facilitating: seminars on psychology, discussion on different subjects, presentation of new youth magazines, concerts, literature parties, theater performances, fashion shows, health clubs, aerobics, arts, exhibitions, excursions, computer clubs, cafes, libraries, sports clubs, meeting clubs, and hairdresser, stylist and make-up training.

We have received many letters from the teenagers as well as the teachers thanking us for the changes that are coming in the students' lives. Everyone—both teachers and students—want us to help them more. The students write that the lessons we are teaching them are necessary, enabling them to see what their problems are, and now they are getting rid of them.

They are starting to think about their position and role in society. They are trying to understand their parents and they are not being selfish anymore. They are seeing how wonderful life really is, and how important it is to respect their elders. They have learned to love people and not look for the defects in others. They write that they understand that "whatever a man sows, he also reaps" is a reality of life. They tell us that they have started thinking more about people, have learned more about friendship, and one student shares that "I was able to tell my mother how much I loved her."

The teachers explain that they are so thankful for the lectures. They write that the presentation on drug addiction influences the students greatly. One teacher reflected, "You made them feel pain, compassion, and disgust, and each of our pupils has vowed to himself not to choose this way of life. Thank you for teaching our students how to find real friends." Both students and teachers wish to continue cooperation with our school ministry. The social services center for youth of the Kiev region thanked us for our lectures to help children socially.

The vision of our school ministry is to raise up the future generation of Kiev students to live according to the principles of the kingdom of God. This vision has three goals: to bring God to pupils from all the schools in Kiev and Kiev region and the other regions, witnessing about His glory in our lives; to help the pupils with their needs and problems; and to teach the students how to achieve and fulfill God's will and calling in their lives.

THE HIGH CALLING OF GOD

The Lord is Almighty. He has called us to take dominion and to instruct the culture. When I gave my life to the Lord, I made a decision neither to condemn other people nor myself. I made a decision to love people, whoever they are, and to expect nothing from them. I made a decision to seek for the kingdom of God and its truth. I decided to depend on no one, except God. I made a decision that no difficulties or tests would stop me from fulfilling my calling. I made a decision to move with God to overcome all obstacles in my way. I made a decision to be one of those whom God will use for His glory and to do my best not to disappoint Him.

If you are faithful in the small things, God says that He will make you ruler over many things. If we really allow ourselves to be used, the Lord will bless us and He will extend His kingdom to all those we come in contact with.

ဢ⊱⊰ဌ

Tatyana's story is a testimony to the power of Christ's resurrection—an example of the "new race" of people born of Jesus the Second Adam—His new creation. Tatyana's testimony shows us how one individual, who is dedicated to obey the Lord and serious about bringing His kingdom on earth, can change her nation and the world.

chapter 19

TODAY'S THE DAY!

You did not choose Me, but I chose you and appointed you
that you should go and bear fruit, and *that* your fruit should
remain, that whatever you ask the Father in My name He may
give you.

—JESUS

JOHN 15:16

One of the greatest lessons I ever learned in my life was from
my dad. From the time I was a very small child and could talk, my
dad would tell me all the time, "Evangeline, I don't have a big Holy
Spirit and you have a little Holy Spirit—the same Holy Spirit
residing in me is the same Holy Spirit that lives in you. This is the
same Holy Spirit who raised Jesus from the dead, who parted the
Red Sea, who still heals the sick and raises the dead, and who makes
the impossible possible. What God tells you to do is just as important as what He tells me to do, so anytime God speaks to you
anything to share or tells you anything to do, just do it!"

Today, God is calling for an army of those who will believe
that this great Holy Spirit lives in their hearts. He is calling for an
army of Davids who will not allow Goliath to challenge the One
True God, but will instead take the battle to the enemy's territory
and see "the kingdoms of this world become the kingdoms of our
God and of His Christ" (Rev. 11:15). God is looking for those who

will believe in Him, trust in His word, and rely on His promises. He is looking for those who will not hold back because of fear, or because of the unknown, but will fully submit their lives to Him, desire what He desires, will what He wills, and spend their lives being led by His Holy Spirit. These are the ones (male or female) God calls His sons "for as many as are led by the Spirit of God these are the sons of God" (Rom. 8:14).

And you are called to be one of His sons for such a time as this—to bring in the greatest harvest the world has yet to see! Over 30 million of your peers did not live to see the light of day. You were spared by the sovereign grace of God from the abortion mills, and you have already made it through many trials and dangers.

Now, you have come to Christ's kingdom for such a time as this. The hearts of mankind cry out to know the Living God. Jesus wants to shine the light of His salvation on those sitting in chains in places of darkness and misery. It is His will that "the earth is filled with the knowledge of the Lord as the waters cover the sea"(Isa. 11:9). He wants to use you to help fulfill His will (Rev. 11:15).

If we are stubborn or refuse to act, it is possible to lose what Christ would have us gain. This concept is immortalized in scripture through the words of Mordecai as he reminded Esther of the opportunity she had to deliver her people from certain death and the consequences she would face if she refused to act: "For if you remain completely silent at this time, relief and deliverance will arise for the Jews from another place, but you and your father's house will perish. Yet who knows whether you have come to the kingdom for *such* a time as this?" (Esther 4:13-14).

THE TIME FOR CHOOSING

No sadder eulogy could be written than we failed to be all that God called us to be and did not fulfill His will and His purposes for our lives and our generation. If we do not stand up and act in our generation, God will choose another generation to fulfill His purposes, but the cost to each one of us and our children will be tragic.

The time has come to take your place as sons and daughters of the Most High God. There is a line drawn in the sand—choose today whom you will serve. Pick up the sword of the Spirit, which is the Word of God. Become skilled in the Word of the Lord. Know what the Bible teaches, but don't stop there. Spend time in the secret place of the Most High, in the inner sanctuary of your heart in true worship. Listen to the "still small voice" of God's Spirit speaking in your heart. Then step out upon God's word and see His promises become a living reality in your life. Become a co-creator with God toward the establishing of His kingdom purposes.

Like many of the great heroes of faith and the people in this book, you may not feel totally prepared for the call. Paul reminds us that our faith should not rest in the wisdom and power of men, but in the power of God. Always remember, "Faithful is He who calls you, and He will also bring it to pass" (1 Thess. 5:24 NAS). Only God can show you what your purpose is in His kingdom, but when He does—run after it with all your heart!

And always remember that "we are surrounded by a great cloud of witnesses" who have gone before us and are waiting on the other side for us to fulfill our part in the Divine conquest (Heb.12:1). Take a moment and really think about this. Imagine this "great cloud of witnesses." See them standing there in the largest stadium ever known—bigger than all the stadiums you have ever seen all put together. In that audience is every lover of Jesus through the ages that you have ever heard of, and all those you have never heard of— unknown on earth, but in heaven now proclaimed.

Look! There stand the martyrs who gave their lives for the Gospel, who didn't deny Jesus even unto death. There are all the apostles, all the fathers and mothers of the church of Jesus Christ who saw pagan nations smash idols and become disciples of the Living Christ. There are all the great revivalists who introduced people to a personal knowledge of the Lord Jesus, who snatched people from the fires of hell, and all those who worked to free this world from injustice and slavery and changed the courses of nations. All the heroes of faith who gave the time they had on earth to see God's glory and His kingdom established from every age are there— "those of whom the world was not worthy" (Heb.11:38). And now they are all cheering for those whose name God is calling.

All of a sudden you notice that they are looking in your direction. "Who could they be looking at?" you wonder. "Certainly, not me."

As you turn around, you see that you are just the one they are looking at. "Why are they looking at me?" you question. "I have nothing to offer. I am just an ordinary person."

Suddenly, they start shouting your name. They are cheering for you! Believing in you! Can you hear them? "Come on John! Come on Sarah! Come on Nathan! Come on Matthew! Come on Peter! Come on Rebecca! Give the Lamb of God the glory that is due His sufferings!"

They are waiting to see you bring God's kingdom and glory to earth! You may be the only one that can do what God is asking of you in this generation. Will you answer the call? Now you have a decision to make. Are you going to continue with business as usual, living your life and wasting time pursuing your own interests, or are you going to pursue God with everything you have to give? What will you do differently now?

You may be thinking, "I don't know exactly what I have to give—but I want my life to count for something greater than myself. Lord Jesus, I want You to use me like You used the great heroes of the Bible and like You have used the young people in this book."

All you have to say is this —"Lord, I give you all that I am. Do whatever you want to do in me and through me for Your Glory."

Then ask Jesus what part you are to play in His army for this huge harvest! Ask Him if there is anything He would have you do differently—if there is anything you need to lay down to follow after Him and His plan for His kingdom. Ask Him if there are any changes He would have you make in the way you spend your time. God will give you His heart if you ask Him for it.

If we want to change the world, then the word of God exhorts us to "not be spiritually dull or indifferent" but to be "imitators of those who through faith and patience inherit the promises" (Heb. 6:12 NLT, NLT). Through faith they "subdued kingdoms, worked righteousness, obtained promises, stopped the mouths of lions, quenched the violence of fire, escaped the edge of the sword, out of weakness were made strong, became valiant in battle, turned to flight the armies of the aliens, received their dead raised to life again."

And not only that, they were not afraid to suffer for what they believed. The scriptures speak of the sacrifice of some of these men and women of faith: "Others were tortured, not accepting deliverance, that they might obtain a better resurrection. Still others had trials of mockings and scourgings, yes, and of chains and imprisonment. They were stoned, they were sawn in two, were tempted, were slain with the sword. They wandered about in sheepskins and goatskins, being destitute, afflicted, tormented— of whom the world was not worthy. They wandered in deserts and mountains, in dens and caves of the earth" (Heb. 11:33-38).

If we want to change the world, we are exhorted by the Holy Scriptures to do what they did—"Since we are surrounded by so great a cloud of witnesses, let us lay aside every weight, and the sin which so easily ensnares *us,* and run with endurance the race that is set before us, looking unto Jesus, the author and finisher of *our* faith, who for the joy that was set before Him endured the cross, despising the shame, and has sat down at the right hand of the throne of God" (Heb. 12:1-2).

THE PROMISE OF HARVEST

Luke records that one day Jesus had been teaching the people by Lake Gennesraet. He saw two boats lying on the shore and fishermen were standing beside the boats washing their nets. Jesus got into one of the boats and asked the fisherman to take Him out from the shore so He could teach the people from there. The boat happened to belong to a man called Simon—Jesus would later change his name to Peter.

After Jesus had finished teaching, He told Simon to cast his net into the sea for a catch. Simon objected saying, "Master, we worked hard all night and caught nothing, but I will do as You say and let down the nets." Suddenly he pulled in a catch of fish that was so heavy the nets began to break, so he signaled his partners to come out and help him, and they filled their boats with so many fish that their boats started to sink.

They were all so astonished at this that Simon Peter fell down at Jesus' feet and said, "Master, depart from me because I am a sinful man." But Jesus said to Peter, "Don't be afraid. From now on you'll be catching men!" Luke records for all time what happened to Simon Peter and his friends that day when they came to the time of choosing: "And when they had brought their boats to the shore, they left everything and followed Him" (Luke 5:8-11, Mark 1:17).

To all those Jesus calls, He gives the same promise of harvest that He gave to His disciples over 2000 years ago, "Follow Me, and I will make you fishers of men!" My prayer for you is that you will rise up in the power of the Holy Spirit and answer Christ's call. Fellowship with the Living God, peace within, abundant life, and a lifetime of adventure await you. Heaven is waiting to burst out into the world through you!

end notes

INTRODUCTION
WHY THIS GENERATION IS SO IMPORTANT TO GOD

[1] LB Finer and SK Henshaw, "Estimates of U.S. Abortion Incidence in 2001 and 2002," Alan Guttmacher Institute, 17 May 2005. The Census counted 30,007,094 people in Canada on May 15, 2001. Government of Canada, "Highlights from the 2001 Census of the Population," July 2006 <http://geodepot2.statcan.ca/Diss/Highlights/>.

[2] Isaac Watts, I. From the Christmas carol, "Joy to the World."

CHAPTER 1
ESCAPING THE FATE OF A NOWHERE MAN

[1] William Wordsworth, "Ode to Immortality," *William Wordsworth The Major Works* (New York: Oxford University Press, 1984), 299.

[2] Lady Nancy Astor, "Dream Quotes," Famous Quotes and Famous Sayings Network, 2006 < http://quotations.home.worldnet.att.net/dreams.html>.

[3] T.E. Lawrence, most famous quote from *Seven Pillars of Wisdom, a Triumph,* July 2006 <LucindaCafehttp://www.lucidcafe.com/library/95aug/lawrence.html>.

[4] Walt Disney, "Brainy Quote" <http://www.brainyquote.com/quotes/quotes/w/waltdisney163027.html>.

Chapter 2
The Path of Absolute Surrender

[1] For more information on the Global Children's Movement visit <http://globalchildrensmovement.com>.

Chapter 7
Developing your Friendship with the Lord

[1] Mother Teresa, *The Love of Christ*, (San Francisco: Harper & Row, 1982) 9.

[2] Gregory S. Neal, *Grace Upon Grace*, Chapter 5 <http://www.revneal.org/Writings/holycommunion5.html>.

[3] Phoebe Palmer, *The Way of Holiness*, (Ann Arbor Michigan: University of Michigan Library, 2005) 126 <http://www.hti.umich.edu/cgi/t/text/text-idx?c=moa;idno=AJH1642.0001.001>.

Chapter 8
No Greater Love

[1] Mother Teresa, *The Love of Christ*, (San Francisco: Harper & Row, 1982) 14-15.

Chapter 10
Where Dreams Become Reality

[1] For more information on Regenerate.com visit <www.regeneratecom.co.uk> and for more info on Roe Hampton Community Church visit <www.roechurch.org>.

CHAPTER 11
RECEIVING THE INVISIBLE SUPPLY

[1] Famous Predictions http://www.baetzler.de/humor/predictions.html>.

[2] Med League Support Services, "Top Quotes for the New Year" <http://www.medleague.com/Articles/president/topquotes.htm>.

CHAPTER 12
SUPERNATURAL PROVISION

[1] For more information on Die Arche visit <http://www.arche-chemnitz.de/_start_english.htm>.

CHAPTER 13
THE POWER OF YOUR THOUGHTS

[1] James Strong, *The Exhaustive Concordance of the Bible*, "Greek Dictionary of the New Testament" 2588 (Nashville: Abbington Press, 1973) 39.

[2] Dr. Robert Schuller, *The Hour of Power,* television production, 2005.

[3] Joseph Goodwin Terrill, The *Life of John Wesley Redfield*, Chapter 14, Christian Classics Ethereal Library <http://www.ccel.org/ccel/terrill_jg/redfield.xix.html>.

[4] Dr. David Yonggi Cho, *The Fourth Dimension,* Vol. 2 (Brunswick, New Jersey: Bridge-Logos, 1983), 17-18.

[5] Ibid, 20-25.

[6] Walt Disney, "Brainy Quote"
<http://www.brainyquote.com/quotes/authors/w/walt_disney.html>.

CHAPTER 15
A REVELATION OF JESUS CHRIST

[1] Jonathan Edwards, *The Works of Jonathan Edwards Vol. 1* (Carlisle, Penn.: Banner pf Truth Trust, 1979), 608. 618.

[2] For more information about Kamron, visit his web site at <www.holyspiritadventures.org>

CHAPTER 16
A NEW MINDSET

[1] Ralph Woodrow, *Great Prophecies of the Bible* (Palm Springs: Woodrow, 1989), 156-173.

[2] *The Holy Bible Clarified Edition,* "Letter to King James" (Chicago: Consolidated Book Publishers, 1971),v.

[3] Jonathan Edwards, *The Works of Jonathan Edwards Vol. 1* (Carlisle, Penn.: Banner pf Truth Trust, 1979), 599.

[4] William Bradford, *The History of Plymouth Plantation*, Chapter 1 < http://members.aol.com/calebj/bradford_journal1.html>.

[5] Ibid, Chapter 4.

[6] Ibid, Chapter 1.

[7] Iain H. Murray, *The Puritan Hope* (Carlisle, Penn: Banner of Truth Trust, 1975), xiv.

[8] Ronald E, Vallet, *Stepping Stones of the Steward: A Faith Journey through Jesus' Parables* (Wm. B. Eerdman Pub., 1994), 75.

[9] Keith Greene, *Ultimate Collection CD*.

[10] Terry D. Bilhartz, *Francis Asbury's America* (Grand Rapids, Michigan: Francis Asbury Press, Zondervan Pub.,1984), 121.

[11] Woodrow Wilson, "John Wesley's Place in History" <http://www.sacred-texts.com/chr/wesplc.htm>.